The Destiny of the Soul

Vol IV

PART FOURTH

CHRISTIAN THOUGHTS CONCERNING A FUTURE LIFE.

CHAPTER I.

PATRISTIC DOCTRINE OF A FUTURE LIFE.

WITH reference to the present subject, we shall consider the period of the Church Fathers as including the nine centuries succeeding the close of the apostolic age. It extends from Clement, Barnabas, and Hermas to OEcumenius and Gerbert.

The principal components of the doctrine of the future life held during this period, though showing some diversities and changes, are in their prevailing features of one consistent type, constituting the belief which would in any of those centuries have been generally recognised by the Church as orthodox.

For reasons previously given, we believe that Jesus himself taught a purely moral doctrine concerning the future life, a doctrine free from arbitrary, mechanical, or sacerdotal peculiarities. With experimental knowledge, with inspired insight, with fullest authority, he set forth conclusions agreeing with the wisest philosophy and confirmatory of our noblest hopes, namely, that a conscious immortality awaits the soul in the many mansions of the Father's house, which it enters on leaving the body, and where its experience will depend upon ethical and spiritual conditions. To this simple and sublime doctrine announced by Jesus, so rational and satisfactory, we believe for reasons already explained that the apostles joined various additional and modifying notions, Judaic and Gentile, such as the local descent of Christ into the prison world of the dead, his mission there, his visible second coming, a bodily resurrection, a universal scenic judgment, and other kindred views. The sum of results thus reached the Fathers developed in greater detail, distinguishing and emphasizing them, and also still further corrupting them with some additional conceptions and fancies, Greek and Oriental, speculative and imaginative. The peculiar theological work of the apostles in regard to this subject was the organizing of the Persian Jewish doctrine of the Pharisees, with a Christian complement and modifications, around the person of Christ, and fixing so near in the immediate future the period when it was to be consummated that it might be looked for at any time. The peculiar theological work of the

Fathers in regard to the doctrine thus formed by the apostles was twofold. First, being disappointed of the expected speedy second coming of Christ, they developed the intermediate state of the dead more fully, and made it more prominent. Secondly, in the course of the long and vehement controversies which sprang up, they were led to complete and systematize their theology, to define their terms, to explain and defend their doctrines, comparing them together and attempting to harmonize them with history, reason, and ethics, as well as with Scripture and tradition. In this way the patristic mind became familiar with many processes of thought, with many special details, and with some general principles, quite foreign to the apostolic mind. Meanwhile, defining and systematizing went on, loose notions hardened into rigid dogmas, free thought was hampered by authority, the scheme generally received assumed the title of orthodox, anathematizing all who dared to dissent, and the fundamental outlines of the patristic eschatology were firmly established.1

In seeking to understand and to give an exposition of this scheme of faith, we have, besides various collateral aids, three chief guidances. First, we possess the symbols or confessions of faith put forth by several of the leading theologians of those times, or by general councils, and openly adopted as authority in many of the churches, the creed falsely called the Apostles', extant as early as the close of the third century, the creed of Arius, that of Cyril, the Nicene creed, the creed falsely named the Athanasian, and others. Secondly, we have the valuable assistance afforded by the treatises of Irenaus, Tertullian, Epiphanius, Augustine, and others still later, on the heresies that had arisen in the Church, treatises which make it easy to infer, by contrast and construction, what was considered orthodox from the statement of what was acknowledged heretical. And, thirdly, abundant resources are afforded us in the extant theological dissertations, and historical documents of the principal ecclesiastical authors of the time in review, a cycle of well known names, sweeping from

Theophilus of Antioch to Photius of Byzantium, from Cyprian of Carthage to Maurus of Mentz. We think that any candid person, mastering these sources of information in the illustrating and discriminating light of a sufficient knowledge of the previous and the succeeding related opinions, will recognise in the following abstract a fair representation of the doctrine of a future life as it was held by the orthodox Fathers of the Christian Church in the period extending from the first to the tenth century.

Before proceeding to set forth the common patristic scheme, a few preliminary remarks are necessary in relation to some of the peculiar, prominent features of Origen's theology, and in relation to the rival systems of Augustine and Pelagius. Origen was a man of vast learning, passionately fond of philosophy; and he modifyingly mingled a great many Oriental and Platonic notions with his theology. He imagined that innumerable worlds like this had existed and perished before it, and that innumerable others will do so after it in endless succession.2 He held that all souls whether devils, men, angels, or of whatever rank were of the same nature; that all who exist in material bodies are imprisoned in them as a punishment for sins committed in a previous state; the fig leaves in which Adam and Eve were dressed after their sin were the fleshly bodies they were compelled to assume on being expelled from the Paradise of their previous existence; that in proportion to their sins they are confined in subtile or gross bodies of adjusted grades until by penance and wisdom they slowly win their

1 Bretschneider, Was lehren die altesten Kirchenvater uber die Entstehung der Sude und des Todes, Adam's Vergehen und die Versohnung durch Christum. Oppositionsschrift, band viii. hft. 3, ss. 380-407.

2 De Principiis, lib. lit. cap. 5.

deliverance, this gradual descent and ascent of souls being figuratively represented by Jacob's ladder; that all punishments and rewards are exactly fitted to the degree of sin or merit, without possibility of failure; that all suffering even that in the lowest hell is benevolent and remedial, so that even the worst spirits, including Satan himself, shall after a time be restored to heaven; that this alternation of fall and restoration shall be continued so often as the cloy and satiety of heavenly bliss, or the preponderant power of temptation, pervert free will into sin.3 He declared that it was impossible to explain the phenomena and experience of human life, or to justify the ways of God, except by admitting that souls sinned in a pre existent state. He was ignorant of the modern doctrine of vicarious atonement, considered as placation or satisfaction, and regarded Christ's suffering not as a substitute for ours, but as having merely the same efficacy in kind as the death of any innocent person, only more eminent in degree. He represents the mission of Christ to be to show men that God can forgive and recall them from sin, banishment, and hell, and to furnish them, in various ways, helps and incitements to win salvation. The foregoing assertions, and other kindred points, are well established by Mosheim, in his exposition of the characteristic views of Origen.4

The famous controversy between Augustine and Pelagius shook Christendom for a century and a half, and has rolled its echoing results even to the theological shores of to day. Augustine was more Calvinistic in his doctrines than the Fathers before him, and even than most of those after him. In a few particulars perhaps a majority of the Fathers really agreed more nearly with Pelagius than with him. But his system prevailed, and was publicly adopted for all Christendom by the third general council at Ephesus in the year 431. Yet some of its principles, in their full force, were actually not accepted. For instance, his dogma of unconditional election that some were absolutely predestinated to eternal salvation, others to eternal damnation has never been taught by the Roman Catholic Church. When

Gottschalk urged it in the ninth century, it was condemned as a heresy;5 and among the Protestants in the sixteenth century Calvin was obliged to fight for it against odds. Augustine's belief must therefore be taken as a representation of the general patristic belief only with caution and with qualifications. The distinctive views of Augustine as contrasted with those of Pelagius were as follow.6 Augustine held that, by Adam's fault, a burden of sin was entailed on all souls, dooming them, without exception, to an eternal banishment in the infernal world. Pelagius denied the doctrine of "original sin," and made each one responsible only for his own personal sins. Augustine taught that baptism was necessary to free its subject from the power which the devil had over the soul on account of original sin, and that all would infallibly be doomed to hell who were not baptized, except, first, the ancient saints, who foreknew the evangelic doctrines and believed, and, secondly, the martyrs, whose blood was their baptism. Pelagius claimed that Christian baptism was only necessary to secure an

3 Ibid. lib. ii. cap. 9, 10.

4 Commentaries on the Affairs of the Christians in the First Three Centuries: Third Century sects. 27-29.

5 Hagenbach, Dogmengeschichte, sect. 183.

6 Wiggers, Augustinism and Pelagianism, trans. from the German by R. Emerson, ch. xix.; also pp. 62, 68, 75, 79.

entrance into heaven: infants and good men, if unbaptized; would enjoy a happy immortality in Paradise, but they never could enter the kingdom of heaven. Augustine affirmed that Adam's sin destroyed the freedom of the will in the whole human race. Pelagius asserted the freedom of the individual will. Augustine declared that a few were arbitrarily elected to salvation from eternity, and that Christ died only for them. Pelagius taught that salvation or reprobation depended on personal deserts, and that the Divine election was merely through prescience of merits. Augustine said that saving grace was supernatural, irresistible, unattainable by human effort. Pelagius said it might be won or resisted by conformity to certain conditions in each person's power. Augustine believed that bodily death was inflicted as a punishment for sin;7 Pelagius, that it was the result of a natural law. The extensive, various learning, massive, penetrating mind, and remorseless logical consistency, of Augustine, enabled him to gather up the loose, floating theological elements and notions of the time, and generalize them into a complete system, in striking harmony, indeed, with the general character and drift of patristic thought, but carried out more fully in its details and applied more unflinchingly in its principles than had been done before, and therefore in some of its dogmas outstripping the current convictions of his contemporaries. His dogma of election was too revolting and immoral ever to win universal assent; and few could have the heart to unite with him in stigmatizing the whole human race in their natural state as "one damned batch and mass of perdition!" (conspersio damnata, massa perditionis.) With these hints, we are ready to advance to the general patristic scheme of eschatology. The exceptional variations and heresies will be referred to afterwards.

First, in regard to the natural state of men under the law, from the time of Adam's sin to the time of Christ's suffering, their moral condition and destination, no one can deny that the Fathers commonly supposed that the dissolution of the body and the descent of the soul to the under world were a penalty brought on all men through the sin of the first man. Wherever the lengthening line of human generations wandered, the trail of the serpent, stamp of depravity, was on them, sealing them as Death's and marking them for the Hadean prison. This was the indiscriminate and the inevitable doom. There is no need of citing proofs of this statement, as it is well known that the writings of the Fathers are thronged both with indirect implications and with explicit avowals of it.

Secondly, they thought that Christ came from heaven to redeem men from their lost state and subterranean bondage and to guide them to heaven. Augustine, and perhaps some others, maintained that he came merely to effectuate the salvation of a foreordained few; but undoubtedly the common belief was that he came to redeem all who would conform to certain conditions which he proposed and made feasible. The important question here is, What did the Fathers suppose the essence of Christ's redemptive work to be? and how, in their estimation, did he achieve that work? Was it the renewal and sanctification of human character by the melting power of a proclamation of mercy and love from God, by the regenerating influences and motives of the truths and appeals spoken by his lips, illustrated

7 In Gen. lib. ix. cap. 10, 11: "Parents would have yielded to children not by death, but by translation, and would have become as the angels."

in his life, and brought to a focus in his martyr death? Certainly this was too plainly and prominently a part of the mission of Christ ever to be wholly overlooked. And yet one acquainted with the writings of the Fathers can hardly mistake so widely as to think that they esteemed this the principal element in Christ's redemptive work. Was the essence of that work, then, the making of a vicarious atonement, according to the Calvinistic interpretation of that phrase, the offering of a substitutional anguish sufficient to satisfy the claims of inexorable justice, so that the guilty might be pardoned? No. The modern doctrine of the atonement the satisfaction theory, as it is called was unknown to the Fathers. It was developed, step by step, after many centuries.8 It did not receive its acknowledged form until it came from the mind of the great Archbishop of Canterbury, Anselm, as late as the twelfth century. No scholar will question this confessed fact. What, then, were the essence and method of Christ's redemptive mission according to the Fathers? In brief, they were these. He was, as they believed, a superangelic being, the only begotten Son of God, possessing a nature, powers, and credentials transcending those delegated to any other being below God himself. He became flesh, to seek and to save the lost. This saving work was done not by his mortal sufferings alone, but by the totality of labors extending through the whole period of his incarnation. The subjective or moral part of his redemptive mission was to regenerate the characters of men and fit them for heaven by his teachings and example; the objective or physical part was to deliver their souls from the fatal confinement of the under world and secure for them the gracious freedom of the sky, by descending himself as the suppressing conqueror of death and then ascending as the beckoning pioneer of his followers. The Fathers did not select the one point or act of Christ's death as the pivot of human redemption; but they regarded that redemption as wrought out by the whole of his humiliation, instruction, example, suffering, and triumph, as the resultant of all the combined acts of his incarnate drama. Run over the relevant writings of Justin Martyr, Clement of Alexandria, Lactantius, Cyril, Ambrose, Augustine himself, Jerome, Chrysostom, and the rest of the prominent authors of the first ten centuries, and you cannot fail to be struck with the fact that they invariably speak of redemption, not in connection with Christ's death alone, but emphatically in connection with the group of ideas, his incarnation, death, descent, resurrection, and ascension! For the most part, they received it by tradition as a fact, without much philosophizing, that, in consequence of the sin of Adam, all men were doomed to die, that is, to leave their bodies and descend into the shadowy realm of death. They also accepted it as a fact, without much attempt at theoretical explanation, that when Christ, the sinless and resistless Son of God, died and went thither, before his immaculate Divinity the walls fell, the devils fled, the prisoners' chains snapped, and the power of Satan was broken. They received it as a fact that through the mediation of Christ the original boon forfeited by Adam was to be restored, and that men, instead of undergoing death and banishment to Hades, should be translated to heaven. So far as they had a theory about the cause, it turned on two simple points: first, the free grace and love of God; second, the self sacrifice and sufficient power of

8 Hagenbach, Dogmengeschichte, sect. 68.

Christ. In the progressive course of dogmatic controversy, metaphysical speculation, and desire for system, explanations have been devised in a hundred different forms, from that of Aquinas to that of Calvin; from that of Anselm to that of Grotius; from that of Socinus to that of Bushnell. Tertullian describes the profound abyss beneath the grave, in the bowels of the earth, where, he says, all the dead are detained unto the day of judgment, and where Christ in his descent made the patriarchs and prophets his companions.9 Augustine says that nearly the whole Church agreed in believing that Christ delivered Adam from the under world when he rose thence himself.10 One must be very ignorant on the subject to doubt that the Fathers attributed unrivalled importance to the literal descent of Christ into the abode of the departed.11

Thirdly, after the advent of Christ, what were the conditions proposed for the actual attainment of personal salvation? It was the orthodox belief that Christ led up into Paradise with him the ancient saints who were awaiting his appearance in the under world:12 but with this exception it was not supposed that he saved any outright: he only put it in their power to save themselves, removing the previously insuperable obstacles. In the faith of those who accepted the dogma of predestination, of course, the presupposed condition of actual personal salvation was that the given individual should become one of the elect number. But it seems to have been usually believed that baptism was indispensable to give final efficacy to the decree of election in each individual case.13 Augustine says, "All are born under the power of the devil, held in chains by him as a jailer: baptism alone, through the force of Christ's redemptive work, breaks these chains and secures heaven." In regard to this necessity of baptism Pelagius agreed with his great adversary, saving an unessential modification, as we have seen before. The same may be said of Cyprian, Tertullian, and many other leading Fathers. Again, the so called Athanasian Creed, which shows the prevalent opinion of the Church in the fifth and sixth centuries, asserts that whoso believes not in the Trinity and kindred dogmas as therein laid down "without doubt shall perish everlastingly." In other words, assent of mind to the established creed of the Church is a vital condition of salvation. Finally, in the writings of nearly all of the Fathers we find frequent declarations of the necessity of moral virtue, righteous conduct, and piety, as a condition of admission into the kingdom of heaven. For example, Augustine says, "Such as have been baptized, partaken of the sacraments, and remained always in the catholic faith, but have led wicked lives, can have no hope of escaping eternal damnation." 14 These points were not sharply defined, authoritatively established, and consistently adhered to; and yet there was a pretty general agreement among the body of the Fathers that for actual salvation there were three practical necessary conditions, baptism, a sound faith, a good life.

9 De Anima, sects. 7 et 55.

10 Epist. CLXIV.

11 Huidekoper, Belief of the First Three Centuries concerning Christ's Mission to the Under World.

12 Augustine, De Civ. Del. lib. xx. cap. xv. Wiedenfeld, De Exorcismi Origine, Mutatione, deque hujus Actus peragendi Ratione Neander, Church

History, vol. i. p. 3

13 Torrey's trans.

14 De Civ. Dei., lib. xxi. cap. xxv.

Fourthly, the Fathers believed that none of the righteous dead could be admitted into heaven itself, the abode of God and his angels, until after the second coming of Christ and the holding of the general judgment; neither were any of the reprobate dead, according to their view, to be thrust into hell itself until after those events; but meanwhile all were detained in an intermediate state, the justified in a peaceful region of the under world enjoying some foretaste of their future blessedness, the condemned in a dismal region of the same under world suffering some foretaste of their future torment.15 After the numerous evidences given in previous chapters of the prevalence of this view among the Fathers, it would be superfluous to cite further authorities here. We will only reply to an objection which may be urged. It may be said, the Fathers believed that Enoch and Elijah were translated to heaven, also that the patriarchs, whom Christ rescued on his descent to Hades, were admitted thither, and, furthermore, that the martyrs by special privilege were granted entrance there. The point is an important one. The reply turns on the broad distinction made by the Fathers between heaven and Paradise. Some of the Fathers regarded Paradise as one division of the under world; some located it in a remote and blessed region of the earth; others thought it was high in the air, but below the dwelling place of God.16 Now, it was to "Paradise," not to heaven, that the dying thief, penitent on the cross, was promised admission. It was of "Paradise," not of heaven, that Tertullian said "the blood of the martyrs is the perfect key." So, too, when Jerome, Chrysostom, and others speak of a few favored ones delivered from the common fate before the day of judgment, it is "Paradise," and not heaven, that is represented as being thrown open to them. Irenaus says, "Those who were translated were translated to the Paradise whence disobedient Adam was driven into the world."17

A notable attempt has been repeatedly made for example, by the famous Dr. Coward, by Dodwell, and by some other more obscure writers to prove that the Fathers of the Greek Church, in opposition to the Latin Fathers, denied the consciousness of the soul during the interval from death to the resurrection, and maintained that the soul died with the body and would be restored with it at the last day. But this is an error arising from the misinterpretation of the figurative terms in which the Greek Fathers express themselves. Tatian, Justin, Theophilus, and Irenaus do not differ from the others in reality, but only in words. The opinion that the soul is literally mortal is erroneously attributed to those Greek Fathers, who in truth no more held it than Tertullian did. "The death" they mean is, to borrow their own language, "deprived of the rays of Divine light, to bear a deathly immortality," (in immortalitate mortem tolerantes,) an eternal existence in the ghostly under world.18 The con

15 They feel, as Novatian says, (De Trinitate, 1,) a prajudicium futuri judicii. See also Ernesti, Excurs. de Veter. Patrum Opinione de Statu Medio Animor. a Corpore sejunctorum. In his Lect. Acad. in Ep. ad Hebr.

16 E. g., see Ambrose, De Paradiso.

17 Adv. Hares., lib. v. cap. v.

18 See this point ably argued in an academic dissertation published at Konigsberg, 1827, bearing the title "Antiquissimorum Ecclesia Grsecte Patrum de Immortalitate Anima Sententia Recensentur."

They held that the inner man was originally a spirit [non-ASCII characters omitted] and a soul [non-ASCII characters omitted] blended and immortal, that is, indestructibly united and blessed. But by sin the soul loses the spirit and becomes subject to death. that is, to ignorance of its Divine origin, alienation from God, darkness, and an abode in Hades. By the influences flowing from the mission of Christ, man is elevated again to conscious communion with God, and the spirit is restored to the soul. "Si restituitur, manet [non-ASCII characters omitted] fit autem [non-ASCII characters omitted]; si non restituitur, manet [non-ASCII characters omitted], fit autem [non-ASCII characters omitted], quod haud differt a morte." cordant doctrine of the Fathers as to the intermediate state of the dead was that, with the exception of a few admitted to Paradise, they were in the under world waiting the fulness of time, when the world should be judged and their final destination be assigned to them. As Tertullian says, "constituimus omnem animam apud inferos seguestrari in diem Domini."

Finally, the Fathers expected that Christ would return from heaven, hold a general day of judgment, and consummate all things. The earliest disciples seem to have looked anxiously, almost from hour to hour, for that awful crisis. But, as years rolled on and the last apostle died, and it came not, the date was fixed more remotely; and, as other years passed away, and still no clear signs of its arrival appeared, the date grew more and more indefinite. Some still looked for the solemn dawn speedily to break; others assigned it to the year 1000; others left the time utterly vague; but none gave up the doctrine. All agreed that sooner or later a time would come when the deep sky would open, and Christ, clothed in terrors and surrounded by pomp of angels, would alight on the globe, when:

"The angel of the trumpet Shall split the charnel earth With his blast so clear and brave, And quicken the charnel birth At the roots of the grave, Till the dead all stand erect."

Augustine, representing the catholic faith, says, "The coming of Elias, the conversion of the Jews, Antichrist's persecution, the setting up of Christ's tribunal, the raising of the dead, the severing of the good and the bad, the burning of the world, and its renovation, this is the destined order of events."19 The saved were to be transported bodily to the eternal bliss of heaven; the damned, in like manner, were to be banished forever to a fiery hell in the centre of the earth, there to endure uncomprehended agonies, both physical and spiritual, without any respite, without any end. There were important, and for a considerable period quite extensive, exceptions, to the belief in this last dogma: nevertheless, such was undeniably the prevailing view, the orthodox doctrine, of the patristic Church. The strict literality with which these doctrines were held is strikingly shown in Jerome's artless question: "If the dead be not raised with flesh and bones, how can the damned, after the judgment, gnash their teeth in hell?"

During the period now under consideration there were great fluctuations, growths, changes, of opinion on three subjects in regard to which the public creeds did not prevent all freedom of thought by laying down definite propositions. We refer to baptism, the millennium, and purgatory. Christian baptism was first simply a rite of initiation into the Christian religion. Then it became more distinctly a symbol of faith in Christ and in his gospel, and an emblem of a new birth. Next it was imagined to be literally efficacious to

19 De Civ. Del, lib. xx. cap. 30, sect. 5.

personal salvation, solving the chains of the devil, washing off original sin, and opening the door of heaven.20 To trace the doctrine through its historical variations and its logical windings would require a large volume, and is not requisite for our present purpose.

Almost all the early Fathers believingly looked for a millennium, a reign of Christ on earth with his saints for a thousand years. Daille has shown that this belief was generally held, though with great diversities of conception as to the form and features of the doctrine.21 It was a Jewish notion which crept among the Christians of the first century and has been transmitted even to the present day. Some supposed the millennium would precede the destruction of the world, others that it would follow that terrible event, after a general renovation. None but the faithful would have part in it; and at its close they would pass up to heaven. Irenaus quotes a tradition, delivered by Papias, that "in the millennium each vine will bear ten thousand branches, each branch ten thousand twigs, each twig ten thousand clusters, each cluster ten thousand grapes, each grape yielding a hogshead of wine; and if any one plucks a grape its neighbors will cry, Take me: I am better!" This, of course, was a metaphor to show what the plenty and the joy of those times would be. According to the heretics Cerinthus and Marcion, the millennium was to consist in an abundance of all sorts of sensual riches and delights. Many of the orthodox Fathers held the same view, but less grossly; while others made its splendors and its pleasures mental and moral.22 Origen attacked the whole doctrine with vehemence and cogency. His admirers continued the warfare after him, and the belief in this celestial Cocaigne suffered much damage and sank into comparative neglect. The subject rose into importance again at the approaching close of the first chiliad of Christianity, but soon died away as the excitement of that ominous epoch passed with equal disappointment to the hopes and the fears of the believers. A galvanized controversy has been carried on about it again in the present century, chiefly excited by the modern sect of Second Adventists. Large volumes have recently appeared, principally aiming to decide whether the millennium is to precede or to follow the second coming of Christ! 23 The doctrine itself is a Jewish Christian figment supported only by a shadowy basis of fancy. The truth contained in it, though mutilated and disguised, is that when the religion of Christ is truly enthroned over the earth, when his real teachings and life are followed, the kingdom of God will indeed cover the world, and not for a thousand years only, but unimaginable glory and happiness shall fill the dwellings of the successive generations of men forever.24

The doctrine of a purgatory a place intermediate between Paradise and hell, where souls not too sinful were temporarily punished, and where their condition and stay were in the power of the Church on earth, a doctrine which in the Middle Age became practically

20 Neander, Planting and Training, Eng. trans. p. 102.

21 De Usu Patrum, lib. ii. cap. 4.

22 Munscher, Entwickelung der Lehre vom Tausendjahrigen Reiche in den Drei Ersten Jahrhunderten. In Henke's Magaz. b. vi. ss. 233 254.

23 See e. g. The End, by Dr. Cumming. The Second Advent, by D. Brown.

24 Bush, On the Millennium. Bishop Russell, Discourses on the Millennium. Carroll, Geschichte des Chiliasmus.

the foremost instrument of ecclesiastical influence and income was through the age of the Fathers gradually assuming shape and firmness. It seems to have been first openly avowed as a Church dogma and effectively organized as a working power by Pope Gregory the Great, in the latter part of the sixth century.25 No more needs to be said here, as the subject more properly belongs to the next chapter.

It but remains in close to notice those opinions relating to the future life which were generally condemned as heresies by the Fathers. One of the earliest of these was the destruction of the intermediate state and the denial of the general judgment by the assertion, which Paul charges so early as in his day upon Hymeneus and Philetus, "that the resurrection has passed already;" that is, that the soul, when it leaves the body, passes immediately to its final destination. This opinion reappeared faintly at intervals, but obtained very little prevalence in the early ages of the Church. Hierax, an author who lived at Leontopolis in Egypt early in the fourth century, denied the resurrection of the body, and excluded from the kingdom of heaven all who were married and all who died before becoming moral agents.

Another heretical notion which attracted some attention was the opposite extreme from the foregoing, namely, that the soul totally dies with the body, and will be restored to life with it in the general resurrection at the end of the world; an opinion held by an Arabian sect of Christians, who were vanquished in debate upon it by Origen, and renounced it.26

Still another doctrine known among the Fathers was the belief that Christ, when he descended into the under world, saved and led away in triumph all who were there, Jews, pagans, good, bad, all, indiscriminately. This is number seventy nine in Augustine's list of the heresies. And there is now extant among the writings of Pope Boniface VI, of the ninth century, a letter furiously assailing a man who had recently maintained this "damnable doctrine."

The numerous Gnostic sects represented by Valentinus, Cerinthus, Marcion, Basilides, and other less prominent names, held a system of speculation copious, complex, and of intensely Oriental character. That portion of it directly connected with our subject may be stated in few words. They taught that all souls pre existed in a world of pure light, but, sinning through the instigation and craft of demons, they fell, were mixed with darkness and matter, and bound in bodies. Through sensual lusts and ignorance, they were doomed to suffer after death in hell for various periods, and then to be born again. Jehovah was the enemy of the true God, and was the builder of this world and of hell, wherein he contrives to keep his victims imprisoned by deceiving them to worship him and to live in errors and indulgences. Christ came, they said, to reveal the true God, unmask the infernal character and wiles of Jehovah, rescue those whom he had cruelly shut up in hell, and teach men the real way of salvation. Accordingly, Marcion declared that when Christ descended into the under world he released and took into his own kingdom Cain, and the Sodomites, and all the

25 Flugge, Geschichte der Lehre vom Zustande des Menschen nach dem Tode in der Christlichen Kirche, absch. v. ss. 320-352.

26 Eusebius, Hist. Eccl. lib. vi. cap. 37.

Gentiles who had refused to obey the demon worshipped by the Jews, but left there, unsaved, Abel, Enoch, Noah, Abraham, and the other patriarchs, together with all the prophets.27 The Gnostics agreed in attributing evil to matter, and made the means of redemption to consist in fastings and scourgings of the flesh, with denial of all its cravings, and in lofty spiritual contemplations. Of course, with one accord they vehemently assailed the dogma of the resurrection of the flesh. Their views, too, were inconsistent with the strict eternity of future hell punishments. The fundamental basis of their system was the same as that of nearly all the Oriental philosophies and religions, requiring an ascetic war against the world of sense. The notion that the body is evil, and the cause of evil, was rife even among the orthodox Fathers; but they stopped guardedly far short of the extreme to which the Gnostics carried it, and indignantly rejected all the strange imaginations which those heretics had devised to explain the subject of evil in a systematic manner.28 Augustine said, "If we say all sin comes from the flesh, we make the fleshless devil sinless!" Hermogenes, some of whose views at least were tinged with Gnosticism, believed the abyss of hell was formed by the confluence of matter, and that the devil and all his demons would at last be utterly resolved into matter.29

The theological system of the Manichaan sect was in some of its cardinal principles almost identical with those of the Gnostics, but it was still more imaginative and elaborate.30 It started with the Persian doctrine of two antagonist deities, one dwelling with good spirits in a world of light and love, the other with demons in a realm of darkness and horror. Upon a time the latter, sallying forth, discovered, far away in the vastness of space, the world of light. They immediately assailed it. They were conquered after a terrible struggle and driven back; but they bore with them captive a multitude of the celestial souls, whom they instantly mixed with darkness and gross matter. The good God built this world of mingled light and darkness to afford these imprisoned souls an opportunity to purge themselves and be restored to him. In arranging the material substances to form the earth, a mass of evil fire, with no particle of good in it, was found. It had been left in their flight by the vanquished princes of darkness. This was cast out of the world and shut up somewhere in the dark air, and is the Manichaan hell, presided over by the king of the demons. If a soul, while in the body, mortify the flesh, observe a severe ascetic moral discipline, fix its thoughts, affections, and prayers on God and its native home, it will on leaving the body return to the celestial light. But if it neglect these duties and become more deeply entangled in the toils of depraved matter, it is cast into the awful fire of hell, where the cleansing flames of torture partially purify it; and then it is born again and put on a new trial. If after ten successive births twice in each of five different forms the soul be still unreclaimed, then it is permanently remanded to the furnace of hell. At last, when all the celestial souls seized by the princes of darkness have returned to God, save those just mentioned, this world will be burned. Then the children

27 Irenaus, Adv. Herres., lib. i. cap. 22.

28 Account of the Gnostic Sects, in Moshelm's Comm., II. Century, sect. 65.

29 Lardner, Hist. of Heretics, ch. xviii. sect. 9.

30 Baur, Das Manichaische Religionssystem.

of God will lead a life of everlasting blessedness with him in their native land of light; the prince of evil, with his fiends, will exist wretchedly in their original realm of darkness. Then all those souls whose salvation is hopeless shall be drawn out of hell and be placed as a cordon of watchmen and a phalanx of soldiers entirely around the world of darkness, to guard its frontiers forever and to see that its miserable inhabitants never again come forth to invade the kingdom of light.31

The Christian after Christ's own pattern, trusting that when the soul left the body it would find a home in some other realm of God's universe where its experience would be according to its deserts, capacity, and fittedness, sought to do the Father's will in the present, and for the future committed himself in faith and love to the Father's disposal. The apostolic Christian, conceiving that Christ would soon return to raise the dead and reward his own, eagerly looked for the arrival of that day, and strove that he might be among the saints who, delivered or exempt from the Hadean imprisonment, should reign with the triumphant Messiah on earth and accompany him back to heaven. The patristic Christian, looking forward to the divided under world where all the dead must spend the interval from their decease to the general resurrection, shuddered at the thought of Gehenna, and wrestled and prayed that his tarrying might be in Paradise until Christ should summon his chosen ones, justified from the great tribunal, to the Father's presence. The Manichaan Christian, believing the soul to be imprisoned in matter by demons who fought against God in a previous life, struggled, by fasting, thought, prayer, and penance, to rescue the spirit from its fleshly entanglements, from all worldly snares and illusions, that it might be freed from the necessity of any further abode in a material body, and, on the dissolution of its present tabernacle, might soar to its native light in the blissful pleroma of eternal being.

31 Mosheim, Comm., III. Century, sects. 44-52.

CHAPTER II.

MEDIAVAL DOCTRINE OF A FUTURE LIFE.

THE period of time covered by the present chapter reaches from the close of the tenth century to the middle of the sixteenth, from the first full establishment of the Roman Catholic theology and the last general expectation of the immediate end of the world to the commencing decline of mediaval faith and the successful inauguration of the Protestant Reformation. The principal mental characteristic of that age, especially in regard to the subject of the future life, was fear. "Never," says Michelet, "can we know in what terrors the Middle Age lived." There was all abroad a living fear of men, fear of the State, fear of the Church, fear of God, fear of the devil, fear of hell, fear of death. Preaching consisted very much in the invitation, "Submit to the guidance of the Church while you live," enforced by the threat, "or you shall go to hell when you die." Christianity was practically reduced to some cruel metaphysical dogmas, a mechanical device for rescuing the devil's captives from him, and a system of ritual magic in the hands of a priesthood who wielded an authority of supernatural terrors over a credulous and shuddering laity. It is true that the genuine spirit and contents of Christianity were never wholly suppressed. The love of God, the blessed mediation of the benignant Jesus, the lowly delights of the Beatitudes, the redeeming assurance of pardon, the consoling, triumphant expectation of heaven, were never utterly banished even from the believers of the Dark Age. Undoubtedly many a guilty but repentant soul found forgiveness and rest, many a meek and spotless breast was filled with pious rapture, many a dying disciple was comforted and inspired, by the good tidings proclaimed from priestly lips even then. No doubt the sacred awe and guarded peace surrounding their precincts, the divine lessons inculcated within their walls, the pathetic prayers breathed before their altars, the traditions of saintly men and women who had drawn angelic visitants down to their cells and had risen long ago to be angels themselves, the strains of unearthly melody bearing the hearts of the kneeling crowd into eternity, no doubt these often made cathedral and convent seem "islands of sanctity amidst the wild, roaring, godless sea of the world." Still, the chief general feeling of the time in relation to the future life was unquestionably fear springing from belief, the wedlock of superstitious faith and horror.

During the six centuries now under review the Roman Catholic Church and theology were the only Christianity publicly recognised. The heretics were few and powerless, and the papal system had full sway. Since the early part of the period specified, the working theology of the Roman Church has undergone but few, and, as pertaining to our subject, unimportant, changes or developments. Previous to that time her doctrinal scheme was inchoate, gradually assimilating foreign elements and developing itself step by step. The principal changes now concerning us to notice in the passage from patristic eschatology as deducible, for instance, from the works of

Chrysostom, or as seen in the "Apostles' Creed" to mediaval eschatology as displayed in the "Summa" of Thomas Aquinas or in the Catechism of Trent are these. The supposititious details of the under world have been definitely arranged in greater subdivision; heaven has been opened for the regular admission of certain souls; the loose notions about purgatory have been completed and consolidated; and the whole combined scheme has been organized as a working instrument of ecclesiastical power and profit.

These changes seem to have been wrought out, first, by continual assimilations of Christianity to paganism,1 both in doctrine and ceremony, to win over the heathen; and, secondly, by modifications and growths to meet the exigencies of doctrinal consistency and practical efficiency, exigencies repeatedly arising from philosophical discussion and political opposition.

The degree in which papal Christianity was conformed to the prejudices and customs of the heathen believers, whose allegiance was sought, is astonishing. It extended to hundreds of particulars, from the most fundamental principles of theological speculation to the most trivial details of ritual service. We shall mention only a few instances of this kind immediately belonging to the subject we are treating. In the first place, the hierophant in the pagan Mysteries, and the initiatory rites, were the prototypes of the Roman Catholic bishop and the ceremonies under his direction.2 Christian baptism was made to be the same as the pagan initiation: both were supposed to cleanse from sin and to secure for their subject a better fate in the future life: they were both, therefore, sometimes delayed until just before death.3 The custom of initiating children into the Mysteries was also common, as infant baptism became.4 When the public treasury was low, the magistrates sometimes raised a fund by recourse to the initiating fees of the Mysteries, as the Christian popes afterwards collected money from the sale of pardons.

In the second place, the Roman Catholic canonization was the same as the pagan apotheosis. Among the Gentiles, the mass of mankind were supposed to descend to Hades at death; but a few favored ones were raised to the sky, deified, and a sort of worship paid to them. So the Roman Church taught that nearly all souls passed to the subterranean abodes, but that martyrs and saints were admitted to heaven and might lawfully be prayed to.5

Thirdly, the heathen under world was subdivided into several regions, wherein different persons were disposed according to their deserts. The worst criminals were in the everlasting penal fire of Tartarus; the best heroes and sages were in the calm meadows of Elysium; the hapless children were detained in the dusky borders outside the grim realm of torture; and there was a purgatorial place where those not too guilty were cleansed from their stains. In like manner, the Romanist theologians divided the under world into four parts: hell for the final abode of the stubbornly wicked; one limbo for the painless, contented tarrying of the good patriarchs who died before the advent of Christ had made salvation possible, and another limbo for the sad and pallid resting place of those children who died unbaptized; purgatory, in which expiation is offered in agony for sins committed on earth and unatoned for.6

1 Middleton, Letter from Rome, showing an exact conformity between Popery and Paganism.

2 Lobeck, Aglaophamus, lib. i. sect. 6. Mosheim's Comm., ch. i. sect. 13.

3 Warburton, Div. Leg., book ii. sect. 4.

4 Terence, Phormio, act i scene 1.

5 Council of Trent, sess. vi. can. xxx. Sess. xxv.: Decree on Invocation of Saints.

6 See Milman, Hist. Latin Christianity, book xiv. ch. ii.

Before proceeding further, we must trace the prevalence and progress of the doctrine of purgatory a little as it was known before its embodiment in mediaval mythology, and then as it was embodied there. The fundamental doctrine of the Hindu hell was that a certain amount of suffering undergone there would expiate a certain amount of guilt incurred here. When the disembodied soul had endured a sufficient quantity of retributive and purifying pain, it was loosed, and sent on earth in a new body. It was likewise a Hindu belief that the souls of deceased parents might be assisted out of this purgatorial woe by the prayers and offerings of their surviving children.7 The same doctrine was held by the Persians. They believed souls could be released from purgatory by the prayers, sacrifices, and good deeds of righteous surviving descendants and friends. "Zoroaster said he could, by prayer, send any one he chose to heaven or to hell." 8 Such representations are found obscurely in the Vendidad and more fully in the Bundehesh. The Persian doctrine that the living had power to affect the condition of the dead is further indicated in the fact that, from a belief that married persons were peculiarly happy in the future state, they often hired persons to be espoused to such of their relatives as had died in celibacy.9 The doctrine of purgatory was known and accepted among the Jews too. In the Second Book of Maccabees we read the following account: "Judas sent two thousand pieces of silver to Jerusalem to defray the expense of a sin offering to be offered for the sins of those who were slain, doing therein very well and honestly, in that he was mindful of the resurrection. For if he had not hoped that they who were slain should rise again, it had been superfluous and vain to pray for the dead. Whereupon he made an atonement for the dead, that they might be delivered from sin."10 The Rabbins taught that children by sin offerings could help their parents out of their misery in the infernal world.11 They taught, furthermore, that all souls except holy ones, like those of Rabbi Akiba and his disciples, must lave themselves in the fire river of Gehenna; that therein they shall be like salamanders; that the just shall soon be cleansed in the fire river, but the wicked shall be lastingly burned.12 Again, we find this doctrine prevailing among the Romans. In the great Forum was a stone called "Lapis Manalis," described by Festus, which was supposed to cover the entrance to hell. This was solemnly lifted three times a year, in order to let those souls flow up whose sins had been purged away by their tortures or had been remitted in consideration of the offerings and services paid for them by the living. Virgil describes how souls are purified by the action of wind, water, and fire.13 The feast day of purgatory observed by papal Rome corresponds to the Lemuria celebrated by pagan Rome, and rests on the same doctrinal basis. In the Catholic countries of Europe at the present time, on All Saints' Day, festoons of sweet smelling flowers are hung on the tomb stones, and the people kneeling there repeat the prayer prescribed for releasing the souls of their relatives and friends from the plagues of purgatory. There is a notable coincidence between the Buddhist

7 See references to "Sraddha" in index to Vishnu Purana.

8 Atkinson's trans. of the Shah Nameh, p. 386.

9 Richardson, Dissertation on the Language, Literature, and Manners of the Eastern Nations, p. 347.

10 Cap. xii. 42-45.

11 Eisenmenger, Entdecktes Judenthum, th. ii. kap. vi. s. 357.

12 Kabbala Denudata, tom ii. pars. i. pp. 108, 109, 113.

13 Aneid, lib. vi. 1. 739.

and the Romanist usages. Throughout the Chinese Empire, during the seventh moon of every year, prayers are offered up accompanied by illuminations and other rites for the release of souls in purgatory. At these times the Buddhist priests hang up large pictures, showing forth the frightful scenes in the other world, to induce the people to pay them money for prayers in behalf of their suffering relatives and friends in purgatory.14

Traces of belief in a purgatory early appear among the Christians. Many of the gravest Fathers of the first five centuries naturally conceived and taught, as is indeed intrinsically reasonable, that after death some souls will be punished for their sins until they are cleansed, and then will be released from pain. The Manichaans imagined that all souls, before returning to their native heaven, must be borne first to the moon, where with good waters they would be washed pure from outward filth, and then to the sun, where they would be purged by good fires from every inward stain.15 After these lunar and solar lustrations, they were fit for the eternal world of light. But the conception of purgatory as it was held by the early Christians, whether orthodox Fathers or heretical sects, was merely the just and necessary result of applying to the subject of future punishment the two ethical ideas that punishment should partake of degrees proportioned to guilt, and that it should be restorative. Jeremy Taylor conclusively argues that the prayers for the dead used by the early Christians do not imply any belief in the Papal purgatory.16 The severity and duration of the sufferings of the dead were not supposed to be in the power of the living, either their relatives or the clergy, but to depend on the moral and physical facts of the case according to justice and necessity, qualified only by the mercy of God.

Pope Gregory the Great, in the sixth century, either borrowing some of the more objectionable features of the purgatory doctrine previously held by the heathen, or else devising the same things himself from a perception of the striking adaptedness of such notions to secure an enviable power to the Church, constructed, established, and gave working efficiency to the dogmatic scheme of purgatory ever since firmly defended by the papal adherents as an integral part of the Roman Catholic system.[17] The doctrine as matured and promulgated by Gregory, giving to the representatives of the Church an almost unlimited power over purgatory, rapidly grew into favor with the clergy and sank with general conviction into the hopes and fears of the laity. Venerable Bede, in the eighth century, gives a long account of the fully developed doctrine concerning purgatory, hell, paradise, and heaven. It is narrated in the form of a vision seen by Drithelm, who, in a trance, visits the regions which, on his return, he describes. The whole thing is gross, literal, horrible, closely resembling several well known descriptions given under similar circumstances and preserved in ancient heathen writers.[18] The Church, seeing how admirably this instrument was calculated to promote her interest and deepen her power, left hardly any means untried to enlarge its sweep and intensify its operation. Accordingly, from the ninth to the sixteenth century, no doctrine was so central, prominent, and effective in the common teaching and

14 Asiatic Journal, 1840, p. 210, note.

15 Mosheim, Comm., III. Century, sect. 49, note 3.

16 Dissuasive from Popery, part ii. book ii. sect. 2.

17 Edgar, Variations of Popery, ch. xvi.

18 Hist. Ecc., lib. v. cap. xii. See also lib. iii. cap. xix.

practice of the Church, no fear was so widely spread and vividly felt in the bosom of Christendom, as the doctrine and the fear of purgatory.

The Romanist theory of man's condition in the future life is this, in brief. By the sin of Adam, heaven was closed against him and all his posterity, and the devil acquired a right to shut up their disembodied souls in the under world. In consequence of the "original sin" transmitted from Adam, every human being, besides suffering the other woes flowing from sin, was helplessly doomed to the under world after death. In addition to this penalty, each one must also answer for his own personal sins. Christ died to "deliver mankind from sin," "discharge the punishment due them," and "rescue them from the tyranny of the devil." He "descended into the under world," "subdued the devil," "despoiled the depths," "rescued the Fathers and just souls," and "opened heaven."19 "Until he rose, heaven was shut against every child of Adam, as it still is to those who die indebted." "The price paid by the Son of God far exceeded our debts." The surplus balance of merits, together with the merits accruing from the supererogatory good works of the saints and from the Divine sacrifice continually offered anew by the sacrament of the mass, constituted a reserved treasure upon which the Church was authorized to draw in behalf of any one she chose to favor. The localities of the future life were these:20 Limbus Patrum, or Abraham's Bosom, a place of peace and waiting, where the good went who died before Christ; Limbus Infantum, a mild, palliated hell, where the children go who, since Christ, have died unbaptized; Purgatory, where all sinners suffer until they are purified, or are redeemed by the Church, or until the last day; Hell, or Gehenna, whither the hopelessly wicked have always been condemned; and Heaven, whither the spotlessly good have been admitted since the ascension of Jesus. At the day of judgment the few human souls who have reached Paradise, together with the multitudes that crowd the regions of

"To tell the secrets of their prison house, They could a tale unfold whose lightest word Would harrow up thy soul, freeze thy young blood, Make thy two eyes, like stars, start from their spheres, Thy knotted and combined locks to part, And each particular hair to stand on end Like quills upon the fretful porcupine."

19 Catechism of the Council of Trent.

20 Thomas Aquinas, Summa Theologia, pars Suppl. Quast. 69.

A few specimens of the stories embodying the ideas and superstitions current in the Middle Age may better illustrate the characteristic belief of the time than much abstract description. An unquestioning faith in the personality, visibility, and extensive agency of the devil was almost universal. Ascetics, saints, bishops, peasants, philosophers, kings, Gregory the Great, Martin Luther, all testified that they had often seen him. The mediaval conception of the devil was sometimes comical, sometimes awful. Grimm says, "He was Jewish, heathenish, Christian, idolatrous, elfish, titanic, spectral, all at once." He was "a soul snatching wolf," a "hell hound," a "whirlwind hammer;" now an infernal "parody of God" with "a mother who mimics the Virgin Mary," and now the "impersonated soul of evil."21 The well known story of Faust and the Devil, which in so many forms spread through Christendom, is so deeply significant of the faith and life of the age in which it arose that a volume would be required to unfold all its import. There was an old tradition that the students of necromancy or the black art, on reaching a certain pitch of proficiency, were obliged to run through a subterranean hall, where the devil literally caught the hindmost unless he sped so swiftly that the arch enemy could only seize his shadow, and in that case, a veritable Peter Schlemihl, he never cast a shadow afterwards! A man stood by his furnace one day casting eyes for buttons.

The devil came up and asked what he was doing. "Casting eyes," replied the man. "Can you cast a pair for me?" quoth the devil. "That I can," says the man: "will you have them large or small?" "Oh, very large," answered the devil. He then ties the fiend on a bench and pours the molten lead into his eyes. Up jumps the devil, with the bench on his back, flees howling, and has never been seen since! There was also in wide circulation a wild legend to the effect that a man made a compact with the devil on the condition that he should secure a new victim for hell once in a century. As long as he did this he should enjoy life, riches, power, and a limited ubiquity; but failing a fresh victim at the end of each hundred years his own soul should be the forfeit. He lived four or five centuries, and then, in spite of his most desperate efforts, was disappointed of his expected victim on the last night of the century; and when the clock struck twelve the devil burst into his castle on a black steed and bore him off in a storm of lightning amidst the crash of thunders and the shrieks of fiends. St. Britius once during mass saw the devil in church taking account of the sins the congregation were committing. He covered the parchment all over, and, afraid of forgetting some of the offences, seized the scroll in his teeth and claws to stretch it out. It snapped, and his head was smartly bumped against the wall. St. Britius laughed aloud. The officiating priest rebuked him, but, on being told what had happened, improved the accident for the edification of his hearers.22 On the bursting of a certain glacier on the Alps, it is said the devil was seen swimming down the Rhone, a drawn sword in one hand, a golden ball in the other: opposite the town of Martigny, he cried, "Rise," and instantly the obedient river swelled above its banks and destroyed the town.

Ignes fatui, hovering about marshes and misty places, were thought to be the spirits of unbaptized children endeavoring to guide travellers to the nearest water. A kindred fancy

21 Deutsche Mythologie, cap. xxxiii.: Teufel.

22 Quarterly Review, Jan. 1820: Pop. Myth. of the Middle Ages.

also heard a spectral pack, called "yell hounds," afterwards corrupted to "hell hounds," composed of the souls of unbaptized children, which could not rest, but roamed and howled through the woods all night.23 A touching popular myth said, the robin's breast is so red because it flies into hell with drops of water in its bill to relieve the children there, and gets scorched.

In 1171, Silo, a philosopher, implored a dying pupil of his to come back and reveal his state in the other world. A few days after his death the scholar appeared in a cowl of flames covered with logical propositions. He told Silo that he was from purgatory, that the cowl weighed on him worse than a tower, and said he was doomed to wear it for the pride he took in sophisms. As he thus spoke he let fall a drop of sweat on his master's hand, piercing it through. The next day Silo said to his scholars, "I leave croaking to frogs, cawing to crows, and vain things to the vain, and hie me to the logic which fears not death."

"Linquo coax ranis, cras corvis, vanaque vanis, Ad logicen pergo qua mortis non timet ergo." 24

In the long, quaint poem, "Vision of William concerning Piers Ploughman," written probably by Robert Langland about the year 1362, there are many things illustrative of our subject. "I, Trojanus, a true knight, after death was condemned to hell for dying unbaptized. But, on account of my mercy and truth in administering the laws, the pope wished me to be saved; and God mercifully heard him and saved me without the help of masses."25 "Ever since the fall of Adam, Age has shaken the Tree of Human Life, and the devil has gathered the fruit into hell."26 The author gives a most spirited account of Christ's descent into the under world after his death, his battle with the devils there, his triumph over them, his rescue of Adam, and other particulars.27 In this poem, as in nearly all the extant productions of that period, there are copious evidences of the extent and power of the popular faith in the devil and in purgatory, and in their close connection with the present life, a faith nourishingly embodied in thousands of singular tales. Thomas Wright has collected many of these in his antiquarian works. He relates an amusing incident that once befell a minstrel who had been borne into hell by a devil. The devils went forth in a troop to ensnare souls on earth. Lucifer left the minstrel in charge of the infernal regions, promising, if he let no souls escape, to treat him on the return with a fat monk roasted, or a usurer dressed with hot sauce. But while the fiends were away St. Peter came, in disguise, and allured the minstrel to play at dice, and to stake the souls which were in torture under his care. Peter won, and carried them off in triumph. The devils, coming back and finding the fires all out and hell empty, kicked the hapless minstrel out, and Lucifer swore a big oath that no minstrel should ever darken the door of hell again!

The mediaval belief in a future life was practically concentrated, for the most part, around the ideas of Satan, purgatory, the last judgment, hell. The faith in Christ, God,

23 Allies, Antiquities of Worcestershire, 2d ed. p. 256.

24 Michelet, Hist. de France, livre iv. chap. ix.

25 Vision of Dowell, part iii.

26 Vision of Dobet, part ii.

27 Ibid., part iv.

heaven, was much rarer and less influential. Neander says, "The inmost distinction of mediaval experience was an awful sense of another life and an invisible world." A most piteous illustration of the conjoined faith and fear of that age is furnished by an old dialogue between the "Soul and the Body" recently edited by Halliwell, an expression of humble trust and crouching horror irresistibly pathetic in its simplicity.28 A flood of revealing light is given as to the energy with which the doctrine of purgatory impressed itself on the popular mind, by the two facts, first, that the Council of Auxerre, in 1578, prohibited the administration of the eucharist to the dead; and, secondly, that in the eleventh and twelfth centuries "crosses of absolution" that is, crosses cut out of sheet lead, with the formula of absolution engraved on them were quite commonly buried with the dead.29 The eager sincerity of the mediaval belief in another life is attested, too, by the correspondence of the representations of the dead in their legends to the appearance, disposition, and pursuits they had in life. No oblivious draught, no pure spiritualization, had freed the departed souls from earthly bonds and associations. Light pretexts drew them back to their wonted haunts. A buried treasure allowed them no rest till they had led some one to raise it. An unfinished task, an uncancelled obligation, forced them again to the upper world. In ruined castles the ghosts of knights, in their accustomed habiliments, held tournaments and carousals. The priest read mass; the hunter pursued his game; the spectre robber fell on the benighted traveller.30 It is hard for us now to reproduce, even in imagination, the fervid and frightful earnestness of the popular faith of the Middle Age in the ramifying agency of the devil and in the horrors of purgatory. We will try to do it, in some degree, by a series of illustrations aiming to show at once how prevalent such a belief and fear were, and how they became so prevalent.

First, we may specify the teaching of the Church whose authority in spiritual concerns bore almost unquestioned sway over the minds of more than eighteen generations. By the logical subtleties of her scholastic theologians, by the persuasive eloquence of her popular preachers, by the frantic ravings of her fanatic devotees, by the parading proclamation of her innumerable pretended miracles, by the imposing ceremonies of her dramatic ritual, almost visibly opening heaven and hell to the over awed congregation, by her wonder working use of the relics of martyrs and saints to exorcise demons from the possessed and to heal the sick, and by her anathemas against all who were supposed to be hostile to her formulas, she infused the ideas of her doctrinal system into the intellect, heart, and fancy of the common people, and nourished the collateral horrors, until every wave of her wand convulsed the world. In a pastoral letter addressed to the Carlovingian prince Louis, the grandson of Charlemagne, a letter probably composed by the famous Hincmar, bearing date 858, and signed by the Bishops of Rheims and Rouen, a Gallic synod authoritatively declared that Charles Martel was damned; "that on the opening of his tomb the spectators were affrighted by a smell of fire and the aspect of a horrid dragon, and that a saint of the times was indulged with a pleasant vision of the soul and body of this great hero burning to all eternity in the abyss of hell."

28 Early English Miscellanies, No. 2.

29 London Antiquaries' Archaologis, vol. xxxv. art. 22.

30 Thorpe, Northern Mythology, vol. i., appendix.

A tremendous impulse, vivifying and emphasizing the eschatological notions of the time, an impulse whose effects did not cease when it died, was imparted by that frightful epidemic expectation of the impending end of the world which wellnigh universally prevailed in Christendom about the year 1000. Many of the charters given at that time commence with the words, "As the world is now drawing to a close." 31 This expectation drew additional strength from the unutterable sufferings famine, oppression, pestilence, war, superstition then weighing on the people. "The idea of the end of the world," we quote from Michelet, "sad as that world was, was at once the hope and the terror of the Middle Age. Look at those antique statues of the tenth and eleventh centuries, mute, meager, their pinched and stiffened lineaments grinning with a look of living suffering allied to the repulsiveness of death. See how they implore, with clasped hands, that desired yet dreaded moment when the resurrection shall redeem them from their unspeakable sorrows and raise them from nothingness into existence and from the grave to God."

Furthermore, this superstitious character of the mediaval belief in the future life acquired breadth and intensity from the profound general ignorance and trembling credulousness of that whole period on all subjects. It was an age of marvels, romances, fears, when every landscape of life "wore a strange hue, as if seen through the sombre medium of a stained casement." While congregations knelt in awe beneath the lifted Host, and the image of the dying Savior stretched on the rood glimmered through clouds of incense, perhaps an army of Flagellants would march by the cathedral, shouting, "The end of the world is at hand!" filling the streets with the echoes of their torture as they lashed their naked backs with knotted cords wet with blood; and no soul but must shudder with the infection of horror as the dreadful notes of the "Dies Iioe" went sounding through the air. The narratives of the desert Fathers, the miracles wrought in convent cells, the visions of pillar saints, the thrilling accompaniments of the Crusades, and other kindred influences, made the world a perpetual mirage. The belching of a volcano was the vomit of uneasy hell. The devil stood before every tempted man, Ghosts walked in every nightly dell. Ghastly armies were seen contending where the aurora borealis hung out its bloody banners. The Huns under Attila, ravaging Southern Europe, were thought to be literal demons who had made an irruption from the pit. The metaphysician was in peril of the stake as a heretic, the natural philosopher as a magician. A belief in witchcraft and a trust in ordeals were universal, even from Pope Eugenius, who introduced the trial by cold water, and King James, who wrote volumes on magic, to the humblest monk who shuddered when passing the church crypt, and the simplest peasant who quaked in his homeward path at seeing a will o' the wisp. "Denounced by the preacher and consigned to the flames by the judge, the wizard received secret service money from the Cabinet to induce him to destroy the hostile armament as it sailed before the wind." As a vivid writer has well said, "A gloomy mist of credulity enwrapped the cathedral and the hall of justice, the cottage and the throne. In the dank shadows of the universal ignorance a thousand superstitions, like foul animals of night, were propagated and nourished."

31 Hallam, Middle Ages, ch. ix.

The beliefs and excitements of the mediaval period partook of a sort of epidemic character, diffusing and working like a contagion.32 There were numberless throngs of pilgrims to famous shrines, immense crowds about the localities of popular legends, relics, or special grace. In the magnetic sphere of such a fervid and credulous multitude, filled with the kindling interaction of enthusiasm, of course prodigies would abound, fables would flourish, and faith would be doubly generated and fortified. In commemoration of a miraculous act of virtue performed by St. Francis, the pope offered to all who should enter the church at Assisi between the eve of the 1st and the eve of the 2d of August each year that being the anniversary of the saint's achievement a free pardon for all the sins committed by them since their baptism. More than sixty thousand pilgrims sometimes flocked thither on that day. Every year some were crushed to death in the suffocating pressure at the entrance of the church. Nearly two thousand friars walked in procession; and for a series of years the pilgrimage to Portiuncula might have vied with that to the temple of Juggernaut.33

Nothing tends more to strengthen any given belief than to see it everywhere carried into practice and to act in accordance with it. Thus was it with the mediaval doctrine of the future life. Its applications and results were constantly and universally thrust into notice by the sale of indulgences and the launching of excommunications. Early in the ninth century, Charlemagne complained that the bishops and abbots forced property from foolish people by promises and threats: "Suadendo de coelestis regni beatitudine, comminando de oeterno supplicio inferni."34 The rival mendicant orders, the Franciscans and the Dominicans, acquired great riches and power by the traffic in indulgences. They even had the impudence to affirm that the members of their orders were privileged above all other men in the next world. Milton alludes to those who credited these monstrous assumptions: "And they who, to be sure of Paradise, Dying, put on the weeds of Dominic, Or in Franciscan think to pass disguised."

The Council of Basle censured the claim of the Franciscan monks that their founder annually descended to purgatory and led thence to heaven the souls of all those who had belonged to his order. The Carmelites also asserted that the Virgin Mary appeared to Simon Stockius, the general of their order, and gave him a solemn promise that the souls of such as left the world with the Carmelite scapulary upon their shoulders should be infallibly preserved from eternal damnation. Mosheim says that Pope Benedict XIV. was an open defender of this ridiculous fiction.35

If any one would appreciate the full mediaval doctrine of the future life, whether with respect to the hair drawn scholastic metaphysics by which it was defended, or with respect to the concrete forms in which the popular apprehension held it, let him read the Divina Commedia of Dante; for it is all there. Whoso with adequate insight and sympathy peruses

32 Hecker, Epidemics of the Middle Ages.

33 Quarterly Review, July, 1819: article on Monachism.

34 Perry, History of the Franks, p. 467.

35 Eccl. Hist., XIII. Century, part ii. ch. 2, sect. 29.

the pages of the immortal Florentine at whom the people pointed as he walked the streets, and said, "There goes the man who has been in hell" will not fail to perceive with what a profound sincerity the popular breast shuddered responsive to ecclesiastical threats and purgatorial woes.

The tremendous moral power of this solitary work lies in the fact that it is a series of terrific and fascinating tableaux, embodying the idea of inflexible poetic justice impartially administered upon king and varlet, pope and beggar, oppressor and victim, projected amidst the unalterable necessities of eternity, and moving athwart the lurid abyss and the azure cope with an intense distinctness that sears the gazer's eyeballs. The Divina Commedia, with a wonderful truth, also reflects the feeling of the age when it was written in this respect, that there is a grappling force of attraction, a compelling realism, about its "Purgatory" and "Hell" which are to be sought in vain in the delineations of its "Paradise." The mediaval belief in a future life had for its central thought the day of judgment, for its foremost emotion terror.36

The roots of this faith were unquestionably fertilized, and the development of this fear quickened, to a very great extent, by deliberate and systematic delusions. One of the most celebrated of these organized frauds was the gigantic one perpetrated under the auspices of the Dominican monks at Berne in 1509, the chief actors in which were unmasked and executed. Bishop Burnet has given an extremely interesting account of this affair in his volume of travels. Suffice it to say, the monks appeared at midnight in the cells of various persons, now impersonating devils, in horrid attire, breathing flames and brimstone, now claiming to be the souls of certain sufferers escaped from purgatory, and again pretending to be celebrated saints, with the Virgin Mary at their head. By the aid of mechanical and chemical arrangements, they wrought miracles, and played on the terror and credulity of the spectators in a frightful manner.37 There is every reason to suppose that such deceptions miracles in which secret speaking tubes, asbestos, and phosphorus were indispensable38 were most frequent in those ages, and were as effective as the actors were unscrupulous and the dupes unsuspicious. Here is revealed one of the foremost of the causes which made the belief of the Dark Age in the numerous appearances of ghosts and devils so common and so intense that it gave currency to the notion that the swarming spirits of purgatory were disembogued from dusk till dawn. So the Danish monarch, revisiting the pale glimpses of the moon, says to Hamlet, "I am thy father's spirit, Doom'd for a certain time to walk the night, And for the day confined to fast in fires, Till the foul crimes done in my days of nature Are burnt and purged away."

36 If any one would see in how many forms the faith in hell and in the devil appeared, let him look over the pages of the "Dictionnaire Infernal," by J. Collin de Plancy.

37 Maclaine's trans, of Mosheim's Eccl. Hist., vol. ii. p. 10, note.

38 Manufactures of the Ancients, pub. by Harper and Brothers, 1845, part iv. ch. 3.

When the shadows began to fall thick behind the sunken sun, these poor creatures were thought to spring from their beds of torture, to wander amidst the scenes of their sins or to haunt the living; but at the earliest scent of morn, the first note of the cock, they must hie to their fire again. Midnight was the high noon of ghostly and demoniac revelry on the earth. As the hour fell with brazen clang from the tower, the belated traveller, afraid of the rustle of his own dress, the echo of his own footfall, the wavering of his own shadow, afraid of his own thoughts, would breathe the suppressed invocation, "Angels and ministers of grace defend us!" as the idea crept curdling over his brain and through his veins, "It is the very witching time of night, When churchyards yawn and hell itself breathes out Contagion to this world."

Working in alliance with the foregoing forces of superstition was the powerful influence of the various forms of insanity which remarkably abounded in the Middle Age. The insane person, it was believed, was possessed by a demon. His ravings, his narratives, were eagerly credited; and they were usually full of infernal visions, diabolical interviews, encounters with apparitions, and every thing that would naturally arise in a deranged and preternaturally sensitive mind from the chief conceptions then current concerning the invisible world.39

The principal works of art exposed to the people were such as served to impress upon their imaginations the Church doctrine of the future life in all its fearfulness, with its vigorous dramatic points. In the cathedral at Antwerp there is a representation of hell carved in wood, whose marvellous elaborateness astonishes, and whose painful expressiveness oppresses, every beholder. With what excruciating emotions the pious crowds must have contemplated the harrowingly vivid paintings of the Inferno, by Orcagna, still to be seen in the Campo Santo of Pisa! In the cathedral at Canterbury there was a window on which was painted a detailed picture of

Christ vanquishing the devils in their own domain; but we believe it has been removed. However, the visitor still sees on the fine east window of York Cathedral the final doom of the wicked, hell being painted as an enormous mouth; also in the west front of Lincoln Cathedral an ancient bas relief representing hell as a monstrous mouth vomiting flame and serpents, with two human beings walking into it. The minster at Freyburg has a grotesque bas relief over its main portal, representing the Judgment. St. Nicholas stands in the centre, and the Savior is seated above him. On the left, an angel weighs mankind in a huge pair of scales, and a couple of malicious imps try to make the human scale kick the beam. Underneath, St. Peter is ushering the good into Paradise. On the right is shown a devil, with a pig's head, dragging after him a throng of the wicked. He also has a basket on his back filled with figures whom he is in the act of flinging into a reeking caldron stirred by several imps. Hell is typified, on one side, by the jaws of a monster crammed to the teeth with reprobates, and Satan is seen sitting on his throne above them. A recent traveller writes from

39 De Boismont, Rational Hist. of Hallucivatious, ch. xiv.

Naples, "The favorite device on the church walls here is a vermilion picture of a male and a female soul, respectively up to the waist [the waist of a soul!] in fire, with an angel over each watering them from a water pot. This is meant to get money from the compassionate to pay for the saying of masses in behalf of souls in purgatory." Ruskin has described some of the church paintings of the Last Judgment by the old masters as possessing a power even now sufficient to stir every sensibility to its depths. Such works, gazed on day after day, while multitudes were kneeling beneath in the shadowy aisles, and clouds of incense were floating above, and the organ was pealing and the choir chanting in full accord, must produce lasting effects on the imagination, and thus contribute in return to the faith and fear which inspired them.

Villani as also Sismondi gives a description of a horrible representation of hell shown at Florence in 1304 by the inhabitants of San Priano, on the river Arno. The glare of flames, the shrieks of men disguised as devils, scenes of infernal torture, filled the night. Unfortunately, the scaffolding broke beneath the crowd, and many spectators were burned or drowned, and that which began as an entertaining spectacle ended as a direful reality. The whole affair is a forcible illustration of the literality with which the popular mind and faith apprehended the notion of the infernal world.

Another means by which the views we have been considering were both expressed and recommended to the senses and belief of the people was those miracle plays that formed one of the most peculiar features of the Middle Age. These plays, founded on, and meant to illustrate, Scripture narratives and theological doctrines, were at first enacted by the priests in the churches, afterwards by the various trading companies or guilds of mechanics. In 1210, Pope Gregory "forbade the clergy to take any part in the plays in churches or in the mummings at festivals." A similar prohibition was published by the Council of Treves, in 1227. The Bishop of Worms, in 1316, issued a proclamation against the abuses which had crept into the festivities of Easter, and gives a long and curious description of them.40 There were two popular festivals, of which Michelet gives a full and amusing description, one called the "Fete of the Tipsy Priests," when they elected a Bishop of Unreason, offered him incense of burned leather, sang obscene songs in the choir, and turned the altar into a dice table; the other called the "Fete of the Cuckolds," when the laymen crowned each other with leaves, the priests wore their surplices wrong side out and threw bran in each others' eyes, and the bell ringers pelted each other with biscuits. There is a religious play by Calderon, entitled "The Divine

Orpheus," in which the entire Church scheme of man's fall the devil's empire, Christ's descent there, and the victorious sequel is embodied in a most effective manner. In the priestly theology and in the popular heart of those times there was no other single particular one tenth part so prominent and vivid as that of Christ's entrance after his death into hell to rescue the old saints and break down Satan's power.41

40 Early Mysteries and Latin Poems of the XII. and XIII. Centuries, edited by Thomas Wright. See the eloquent sermon on this subject preached by Luis de Granada in the sixteenth century. Ticknor's Hist. Spanish Lit., vol. iii. pp. 123-127.

Peter Lombard says, "What did the Redeemer do to the despot who had us in his bonds? He offered him the cross as a mouse trap, and put his blood on it as bait." 42 About that scene there was an incomparable fascination for every believer. Christ laid aside his Godhead and died. The devil thought he had secured a new victim, and humanity swooned in grief and despair. But, lo! the Crucified, descending to the inexorable dungeons, puts on all his Divinity, and suddenly "The captive world awakt, and founde The pris'ner loose, the jailer bounde!" 43

A large proportion of the miracle plays, or Mysteries, turned on this event. In the "Mystery of the Resurrection of Christ" occurs the following couplet: "This day the angelic King has risen, Leading the pious from their prison." 44

The title of one of the principal plays in the Towneley Mysteries is "Extractio Animarum ab Inferno." It describes Christ descending to the gates of hell to claim his own. Adam sees afar the gleam of his coming, and with his companions begins to sing for joy. The infernal porter shouts to the other demons, in alarm, "Since first that hell was made and I was put therein, Such sorrow never ere I had, nor heard I such a din. My heart begins to start; my wit it waxes thin; I am afraid we can't rejoice, these souls must from us go. Ho, Beelzebub! bind these boys: such noise was never heard in hell."

Satan vows he will dash Beelzebub's brains out for frightening him so. Meanwhile, Christ draws near, and says, "Lift up your gates, ye princes, and be ye lifted up, ye everlasting doors, and the King of glory shall come in." The portals fly asunder. Satan shouts up to his friends, "Dyng the dastard down;" but Beelzebub replies, "That is easily said." Jesus and the devil soon meet, face to face. A long colloquy ensues, in the course of which the latter tells the former that he knew his Father well by sight! At last Jesus frees Adam, Eve, the prophets, and others, and ascends, leaving the devil in the lowest pit, resolving that hell shall soon be fuller than before; for he will walk east and he will walk west, and he will seduce thousands from their allegiance. Another play, similar to the foregoing, but much more extensively known and acted, was called the "Harrowing of Hell." Christ and Satan appear on the stage and argue in the most approved scholastic style for the right of possession in the human race. Satan says, "Whoever purchases any thing, It belongs to him and to his children. Adam, hungry, came to me;

42 Sententia, lib. iii. distinctio 19.

43 Hone, Ancient Mysteries.

44 "Resurrexit hodie Rex angelorum Ducitur de tenebris turba piorum."

I made him do me homage: For an apple, which I gave him, He and all his race belong to me." But Christ instantly puts a different aspect on the argument, by replying, "Satan! it was mine, The apple thou gavest him. The apple and the apple tree Both were made by me. As he was purchased with my goods, With reason will I have him." 45

In a religious Mystery exhibited at Lisbon as late as the close of the eighteenth century, the following scene occurs. Cain kicks his brother Abel badly and kills him. A figure like a Chinese mandarin, seated in a chair, condemns Cain and is drawn up into the clouds. The mouth of hell then appears, like the jaws of a great dragon: amid smoke and lightning it casts up three devils, one of them having a wooden leg. These take a dance around Cain, and are very jocose, one of them inviting him to hell to take a cup of brimstone coffee, and another asking him to make up a party at whist. Cain snarls, and they tumble him and themselves headlong into the squib vomiting mouth.

Various books of accounts kept by the trading companies who celebrated these Mysteries of the expenses incurred have been published, and are exceedingly amusing. "Item: payd for kepyng of fyer at hellmothe, four pence." "For a new hoke to hang Judas, six pence." "Item: payd for mendyng and payntyng hellmouthe, two pence." "Girdle for God, nine pence." "Axe for Pilatte's son, one shilling." "A staff for the demon, one penny." "God's coat of white leather, three shillings." The stage usually consisted of three platforms. On the highest sat God, surrounded by his angels. On the next were the saints in Paradise, the intermediate state of the good after death. On the third were mere men yet living in the world. On one side of the lowest stage, in the rear, was a fearful cave or yawning mouth filled with smoke and flames, and denoting hell. From this ever and anon would issue the howls and shrieks of the damned. Amidst hideous yellings, devils would rush forth and caper about and snatch hapless souls into this pit to their doom.46 The actors, in their mock rage, sometimes leaped from the pageant into the midst of the laughing, screaming, trembling crowd. The dramatis personoe included many queer characters, such as a "Worm of Conscience," "Deadman," (representing a soul delivered from hell at the descent of Christ,) numerous "Damned Souls," dressed in flame colored garments, "Theft," "Lying," "Gluttony." But the devil himself was the favorite character; and often, when his personified vices jumped on him and pinched and cudgelled him till he roared, the mirth of the honest audience knew no bounds. For there were in the Middle Age two sides to the popular idea of the devil and of all appertaining to him. He was a soul harrowing bugbear or a rib shaking jest according to the hour and one's

45 Halliwell's edition of the Harrowing of Hell, p. 18.

46 Sharp, Essay on the Dramatic Mysteries, p. 24.

humor. Rabelais's Pantagruel is filled with irresistible burlesques of the doctrine of purgatory. The ludicrous side of this subject may be seen by reading Tarlton's "Jests" and his "Newes out of Purgatorie." 47 Glimpses of it are also to be caught through many of the humorous passages in Shakspeare. Dromio says of an excessively fat and greasy kitchen wench, "If she lives till doomsday she'll burn a week longer than the whole world!" And Falstaff, cracking a kindred joke on Bardolph's carbuncled nose, avows his opinion that it will serve as a flaming beacon to light lost souls the way to purgatory! Again, seeing a flea on the same flaming proboscis, the doughty knight affirmed it was "a black soul burning in hell fire." In this element of mediaval life, this feature of mediaval literature, a terrible belief lay under the gay raillery. Here is betrayed, on a wide scale, that natural reaction of the faculties from excessive oppression to sportive wit, from deep repugnance to superficial jesting, which has often been pointed out by philosophical observers as a striking fact in the psychological history of man.

One more active and mighty cause of the dreadful faith and fear with which the Middle Age contemplated the future life was the innumerable and frightful woes, crimes, tyrannies, instruments of torture, engines of persecution, insane superstitions, which then existed, making its actual life a hell. The wretchedness and cruelty of the present world were enough to generate frightful beliefs and cast appalling shadows over the future. If the earth was full of devils and phantoms, surely hell must swarm worse with them. The Inquisition sat shrouded and enthroned in supernatural obscurity of cunning and awfulness of power, and thrust its invisible daggers everywhere. The facts men knew here around them gave credibility to the imagery in which the hereafter was depicted. The flaming stakes of an Auto da Fe around which the victims of ecclesiastical hatred writhed were but faint emblems of what awaited their souls in the realm of demons whereto the tender mercies of the Church consigned them. Indeed, the fate of myriads of heretics and traitors could not fail to project the lurid vision of hell with all its paraphernalia into the imaginations of the people of the Dark Age. The glowing lava of purgatory heated the soil they trod, and a smell of its sulphur surcharged the air. A stupendous revelation of terror, bearing whole volumes of direful meaning, is given in the single fact that it was a common belief of that period that the holy Inquisitors would sit with Christ in the judgment at the last day.48 If king or noble took offence at some uneasy retainer or bold serf, he ordered him to be secretly buried in the cell of some secluded fortress, and he was never heard of more. So, if pope or priest hated or feared some stubborn thinker, he straightway, "Would banish him to wear a burning chain In the great dungeons of the unforgiven, Beneath the space deep castle walls of heaven."

It was an age of cruelty, never to be restored, when the world was boiling in tempest and men rode on the crests of fear.

47 Recently edited by Halliwell and published by the Shakspeare Society.

48 Hagenbach, Dogmengeschichte, sect. 205.

Researches made within the last century among the remains of famous mediaval edifices, both ecclesiastic and state, have brought to light the dismal records of forgotten horrors. In many a royal palace, priestly building, and baronial castle, there were secret chambers full of infernal machinery contrived for inflicting tortures, and under them concealed trap doors opening into rayless dungeons with no outlet and whose floors were covered with the mouldering bones of unfortunate wretches who had mysteriously disappeared long ago and tracelessly perished there. Sometimes these trap doors were directly above profound pits of water, in which the victim would drown as he dropped from the mangling hooks, racks, and pincers of the torture chamber. There were horrible rumors current in the Middle Age of a machine called the "Virgin," used for putting men to death; but little was known about it, and it was generally supposed to be a fable, until, some years ago one of the identical machines was discovered in an old Austrian castle. It was a tall wooden woman, with a painted face, which the victim was ordered to kiss. As he approached to offer the salute, he trod on a spring, causing the machine to fly open, stretch out a pair of iron arms, and draw him to its breast covered with a hundred sharp spikes, which pierced him to death.[49]

Ignorance and alarm, in a suffering and benighted age, surrounded by sounds of superstition and sights of cruelty, must needs breed and foster a horrid faith in regard to the invisible world. Accordingly, the common doctrine of the future life prevailing in Christendom from the ninth century till the sixteenth was as we have portrayed it. Of course there are exceptions to be admitted and qualifications to be made; but, upon the whole, the picture is faithful. Fortunately, intellect and soul could not slumber forever, nor the mediaval nightmares always keep their torturing seat on the bosom of humanity. Noble men arose to vindicate the rights of reason and the divinity of conscience. The world was circumnavigated, and its revolution around the sun was demonstrated. A thousand truths were discovered, a thousand inventions introduced. Papacy tottered, its prestige waned, its infallibility sunk. The light of knowledge shone, the simplicity of nature was seen, and the benignity of God was surmised. Thought, throwing off many restrictions and accumulating much material, began to grow free, and began to grow wise. And so, before the calm, steady gaze of enlightened and cheerful reason, the live and crawling smoke of hell, which had so long enwreathed the mind of the time with its pendent and breathing horrors, gradually broke up and dissolved, "Like a great superstitious snake, uncurled From the pale temples of the awakening world."

49 The Kiss of the Virgin, in the Archaologia published by the Antiquaries of London, vol. xxviii.

CHAPTER III.

MODERN DOCTRINE OF A FUTURE LIFE.

THE folly and paganism of some of the Church dogmas, the rapacious haughtiness of its spirit, the tyranny of its rule, and the immoral character of many of its practices, had often awakened the indignant protests and the determined opposition of men of enlightened minds, vigorous consciences, and generous hearts, both in its bosom and out of it. Many such men, vainly struggling to purify the Church from its iniquitous errors or to relieve mankind from its outrageous burdens, had been silenced and crushed by its relentless might. Arnold, Wickliffe, Wessel, Savonarola, and a host of others, are to be gratefully remembered forever as the heroic though unsuccessful forerunners of the mighty monk of Wittenberg.1 The corruption of the mediaval Church grew worse, and became so great as to stir a very extensive disgust and revulsion. Wholesale pardons for all their sins were granted indiscriminately to those who accepted the terms of the papal officials; while every independent thinker, however evangelical his faith and exemplary his character, was hopelessly doomed to hell. Especially were these pardons given to pilgrims and to the Crusaders. Bernard of Clairvaux, exhorting the people to undertake a new Crusade, tells them that "God condescends to invite into his service murderers, robbers, adulterers, perjurers, and those sunk in other crimes; and whosoever falls in this cause shall secure pardon for the sins which he has never confessed with contrite heart."2 At the opening of "Piers the Ploughman's Crede" a person is introduced saying, "I saw a company of pilgrims on their way to Rome, who came home with leave to lie all the rest of their lives!" Nash, in his "Lenten Stuff," speaks of a proclamation which caused "three hundred thousand people to roam to Rome for purgatorie pills." Ecclesiasticism devoured ethics. Allegiance to morality was lowered into devotion to a ritual. The sale of indulgences at length became too impudent and blasphemous to be any longer endured, when John Tetzel, a Dominican monk, travelled over Europe, and, setting up his auction block in the churches, offered for sale those famous indulgences of Leo X. which promised, to every one rich enough to pay the requisite price, remission of all sins, however enormous, and whether past, present, or future!3 This brazen but authorized charlatan boasted that "he had saved more souls from hell by the sale of indulgences than St. Peter had converted to Christianity by his preaching." He also said that "even if any one had ravished the Mother of God he could sell him a pardon for it!" The soul of Martin Luther took fire. The consequence to which a hundred combining causes contributed was the Protestant Reformation. This great movement produced, in relation to our subject, three important results. It noticeably modified the practice and the popular preaching of the Roman Catholic Church.

1 Ullmann, Reformatoren vor der Reformation.

2 Epist. CCCLXIII. ad Orientalis Francia Clerum et Populum.

3 D'Aubigne, Hist. Reformation, book iii.

The dogmas of the Romanist theology remained as they were before. But a marked change took place in the public conduct of the papal functionaries. Morality was made more prominent, and mere ritualism less obtrusive. Comparatively speaking, an emphasis was taken from ecclesiastic confession and indulgence, and laid upon ethical obedience and piety. The Council of Trent, held at this time, says, in its decree concerning indulgences, "In granting indulgences, the Church desires that moderation be observed, lest, by excessive facility, ecclesiastical discipline be enervated." Imposture became more cautious, threats less frequent and less terrible; the teeth of persecution were somewhat blunted; miracles grew rarer; the insufferable glare of purgatory and hell faded, and the open traffic in forgiveness of sins, or the compounding for deficiencies, diminished. But among the more ignorant papal multitudes the mediaval superstition holds its place still in all its virulence and grossness. "Heaven and hell are as much a part of the Italian's geography as the Adriatic and the Apennines; the Queen of Heaven looks on the streets as clear as the morning star; and the souls in purgatory are more readily present to conception than the political prisoners immured in the dungeons of Venice."

A second consequence of the Reformation is seen in the numerous dissenting sects to which its issues gave rise. The chief peculiarities of the Protestant doctrines of the future life are embodied in the four leading denominations commonly known as Lutheran, Calvinistic, Unitarian, and Universalist. Each of these includes a number of subordinate parties bearing distinctive names, (such as Arminian, Presbyterian, Methodist, Baptist,

Restorationist, and many others;) but these minor differences are too trivial to deserve distinctive characterization here. The Lutheran formula is that, through the sacrifice of Christ, salvation is offered to all who will accept it by a sincere faith. Some will comply with these terms and secure heaven; others will not, and so will be lost forever. Luther's views were not firmly defined and consistent throughout his career; they were often obscure, and they fluctuated much. It is true he always insisted that there was no salvation without faith, and that all who had faith should be saved. But, while he generally seems to believe in the current doctrine of eternal damnation, he sometimes appears to encourage the hope that all will finally be saved. In a remarkable letter to Hansen von Rechenberg, dated 1522, he says, in effect, "Whoso hath faith in Christ shall be saved. God forbid that I should limit the time for acquiring this faith to the present life! In the depths of the Divine mercy, there may be opportunity to win it in the future state."

The Calvinistic formula is that heaven is attainable only for those whom the arbitrary predestination of God has elected; all others are irretrievably damned. Calvin was the first Christian theologian who succeeded in giving the fearful doctrine of unconditional election and reprobation a lodgment in the popular breast. The Roman Catholic Church had earnestly repudiated it. Gotteschalk was condemned and died in prison for advocating it, in the ninth century. But Calvin's character enabled him to believe it, and his talents and position gave great weight to his advocacy of it, and it has since been widely received. Catholicism, Lutheranism, Calvinism, all agreed in the general proposition that by sin physical death came into the world, heaven was shut against man, and all men utterly lost. They differed only in some unessential details concerning the condition of that lost state. They also agreed in the general proposition that Christ came, by his incarnation, death, descent to hell, resurrection, and ascension, to redeem men from their lost state. They only differed in regard to the precise grounds and extent of that redemption. The Catholic said, Christ's atonement wiped off the whole score of original sin, and thus enabled man to win heaven by moral fidelity and the help of the Church. The Lutheran said, Christ's atonement made all the sins of those who have faith, pardonable; and all may have faith. The Calvinist said, God foresaw that man would fall and incur damnation, and he decreed that a few should be snatched as brands from the burning, while the mass should be left to eternal torture; and Christ's atonement purchased the predestined salvation of the chosen few. Furthermore, Lutherans and Calvinists, in all their varieties, agree with the Romanist in asserting that Christ shall come again, the dead be raised bodily, a universal judgment be held, and that then the condemned shall sink into the everlasting fire of hell, and the accepted rise into the endless bliss of heaven.

The Socinian doctrine relative to the future fate of man differed from the foregoing in the following particulars. First, it limited the redeeming mission of Christ to the enlightening influences of the truths which he proclaimed with Divine authority, the moral power of his perfect example, and the touching motives exhibited in his death. Secondly, it asserted a natural ability in every man to live a life conformed to right reason and sound morality, and promised heaven to all who did this in obedience to the instructions and after the pattern of Christ. Thirdly, it declared that the wicked, after suffering excruciating agonies, would be annihilated. Respecting the second coming of Christ, a physical resurrection of the dead, and a day of judgment, the Socinians believed with the other sects.4 Their doctrine scarcely corresponds with that of the present Unitarians in any thing. The dissent of the Unitarian from the popular theology is much more fundamental, detailed, and consistent than that of the Socinian was, and approaches much closer to the Rationalism of the present day.

The Universalist formula every soul created by God shall sooner or later be saved from sin and woe and inherit everlasting happiness has been publicly defended in every age of the Christian Church.5 It was first publicly condemned as a heresy at the very close of the fourth century. It ranks among its defenders the names of Clement of Alexandria, Origen, Gregory of Nazianzus, Gregory of Nyssa, and several other prominent Fathers. Universalism has been held in four forms, on four grounds. First, it has been supposed that Christ died for all, and that, by the infinite efficacy of his redeeming merits, all sins shall be cancelled and every soul be saved. This was the scheme of those early Universalist Christians whom Epiphanius condemns as heretics; also of a few in more modern times. Secondly, it has been thought that each person would be punished in the future state according to the deeds done in the body, each sin be expiated by a proportionate amount of suffering, the retribution of some souls being severe and long, that of others light and brief; but, every penalty being at

4 Flugge gives a full exposition of these points with references to the authorities. Lehre vom Zustande, u. s. f., abth. ii. ss. 243-260.

5 Dietelmaier, Commenti Fanatici [non-ASCII characters omitted] Hist. Antiquar.

length exhausted, the last victim would be restored. This was the notion of Origen, the basis of the doctrine of purgatory, and the view of most of the Restorationists. Thirdly, it has been imagined that, by the good pleasure and fixed laws of God, all men are destined to an impartial, absolute, and instant salvation beyond the grave: all sins are justly punished, all moral distinctions equitably compensated, in this life; in the future an equal glory awaits all men, by the gracious and eternal election of God, as revealed to us in the benignant mission of Christ. This is the peculiar conception distinguishing some members of the denomination now known as Universalists. Finally, it has been believed that the freedom and probation granted here extend into the life to come; that the aim of all future punishment will be remedial, beneficent, not revengeful; that stronger motives will be applied for producing repentance, and grander attractions to holiness be felt; and that thus, at some time or other, even the most sunken and hardened souls will be regenerated and raised up to heaven in the image of God. Almost all Universalists, most Unitarians, and large number of individual Christians outwardly affiliated with other denominations, now accept and cherish this theory.

One important variation from the doctrine of the dominant sects, in connection with the present subject, is worthy of special notice. We refer to the celebrated controversy waged in England, in the first part of the eighteenth century, in regard to the intermediate state of the dead. The famous Dr. Coward and a few supporters labored, with much zeal, skill, and show of learning, to prove the natural mortality of the soul. They asserted this to be both a philosophical truth proved by scientific facts and a Christian doctrine declared in Scripture and taught by the Fathers. They argued that the soul is not an independent entity, but is merely the life of the body. Proceeding thus far on the principles of a materialistic science, they professed to complete their theory from Scripture, without doing violence to any doctrine of the acknowledged religion.6 The finished scheme was this. Man was naturally mortal; but, by the pleasure and will of God, he would have been immortally preserved alive had he not sinned. Death is the consequence of sin, and man utterly perishes in the grave. But God will restore the dead, through Christ, at the day of the general resurrection which he has foretold in the gospel.7 Some of the writers in this copious controversy maintained that previous to the advent of Christ death was eternal annihilation to all except a few who enjoyed an inspired anticipatory faith in him, but that all who died after his coming would be restored in the resurrection, the faithful to be advanced to heaven, the wicked to be the victims of unending torture.8 Clarke and Baxter both wrote with extreme ability in support of the natural immortality and separate existence of the soul. On the other hand, the learned Henry Dodwell cited, from the lore of three thousand years, a plausible body of authorities to show that the soul is in itself but a mortal breath. He also contended, by a singular perversion of figurative phrases from the New Testament and from some of the Fathers, that,

6 Coward, Search after Souls.

7 Hallet, No Resurrection, no Future State.

8 Coward, Defence of the Search after Souls. Dodwell, Epistolary Discourse. Peckard, Observations. Fleming, Survey of the Search after Souls. Law, State of Separate Spirits. Layton, Treatise of Departed Souls.

in counteraction of man's natural mortality, all who undergo baptism at the hands of the ordained ministers of the Church of England the only true priesthood in apostolic succession thereby receive an immortalizing spirit brought into the world by Christ and committed to his successors. This immortalizing spirit conveyed by baptism would secure their resurrection at the last day. Those destitute of this spirit would never awake from the oblivious sleep of death, unless as he maintained will actually be the case with a large part of the dead they are arbitrarily immortalized by the pleasure of God, in order to suffer eternal misery in hell! Absurd and shocking as this fancy was, it obtained quite a number of converts, and made no slight impression at the time. One of the writers in this controversy asserted that Luther himself had been a believer in the death or sleep of the soul until the day of judgment.9 Certain it is that such a belief had at one period a considerable prevalence. Its advocates were called Psychopannychians. Calvin wrote a vehement assault on them. The opinion has sunk into general disrepute and neglect, and it would be hard to find many avowed disciples of it. The nearly universal sentiment of Christendom would now exclaim, in the quaint words of Henry More,

"What! has old Adam snorted all this time Under some senselesse clod, with sleep ydead?" 10

John Asgill printed, in the year 1700, a tract called "An argument to prove that by the new covenant man may be translated into eternal life without tasting death." He argues that the law of death was a consequence of Adam's sin and was annulled by Christ's sacrifice. Since that time men have died only because of an obstinate habit of dying formed for many generations. For his part, he has the independence and resolution to withstand the universal pusillanimity and to refuse to die. He has discovered "an engine in Divinity to convey man from earth to heaven." He will "play a trump on death and show himself a match for the devil!"

While treating of the various Protestant views of the future life, it would be a glaring defect to overlook the remarkable doctrine on that subject published by Emanuel Swedenborg and now held by the intelligent, growing body of believers called after his name. It would be impossible to exhibit this system adequately in its scientific bases and its complicated details without occupying more space than can be afforded here. Nor is this necessary, now that his own works have been translated and are easily accessible everywhere. His "Heaven and Hell," "Heavenly Arcana," "Doctrine of Influx," and "True Christian

9 Blackburne, View of the Controversy Concerning an Intermediate State: appendix. It is probable that the great Reformer's opinion on this point was not always the same. For he says, distinctly, "The first man who died, when he awakes at the last day, will think he has been asleep but an hour" Beste, Dr. M. Luther's Glaubenslehre, cap. iv.: Die Lehre von den Letzen Dingen. Yet. J. S. Muller seems conclusively to prove the truth of the proposition which forms the title of his book, "Dass Luther die Lehre vom Seelenschlafe nie geglaubt habe."

10 The controversy concerning the natural immortality of the soul has within a few years raged afresh. The principal combatants were Dobney, Storrs, White, Morris, and Hinton. See Athanasia, by J. H. Hinton, London, 1849.

Religion," contain manifold statements and abundant illustrations of every thing important bearing on his views of the theme before us. We shall merely attempt to present a brief synopsis of the essential principles, accompanied by two or three suggestions of criticism.

Swedenborg conceives man to be an organized receptacle of truth and love from God. He is an imperishable spiritual body placed for a season of probation in a perishable material body. Every moment receiving the essence of his being afresh from God, and returning it through the fruition of its uses devoutly rendered in conscious obedience and joyous worship, he is at once a subject of personal, and a medium of the Divine, happiness. The will is the power of man's life, and the understanding is its form. When the will is disinterested love and the understanding is celestial truth, then man fulfils the end of his being, and his home is heaven; he is a spirit frame into which the goodness of God perpetually flows, is humbly acknowledged, gratefully enjoyed, and piously returned. But when his will is hatred or selfishness and his understanding is falsehood or evil, then his powers are abused, his destiny inverted, and his fate hell. While in the body in this world he is placed in freedom, on probation, between these two alternatives.

The Swedenborgian universe is divided into four orders of abodes. In the highest or celestial world are the heavens of the angels. In the lowest or infernal world are the hells of the demons. In the intermediate or spiritual world are the earths inhabited by men, and surrounded by the transition state through which souls, escaping from their bodies, after a while soar to heaven or sink to hell, according to their fitness and attraction. In this life man is free, because he is an energy in equilibrium between the influences of heaven and hell. The middle state surrounding man is full of spirits, some good and some bad. Every man is accompanied by swarms of both sorts of spirits, striving to make him like themselves. Now, there are two kinds of influx into man. Mediate influx is when the spirits in the middle state flow into man's thoughts and affections. The good spirits are in communication with heaven, and they carry what is good and true; the evil spirits are in communication with hell, and they carry what is evil and false. Between these opposed and reacting agencies man is in an equilibrium whose essence is freedom. Deciding for himself, if he turns with embracing welcome to the good spirits, he is thereby placed and lives in conjunction with heaven; but if he turns, on the contrary, with predominant love to the bad spirits, he is placed in conjunction with hell and draws his life thence. From heaven, therefore, through the good spirits, all the elements of saving goodness flow sweetly down and are appropriated by the freedom of the good man; while from hell, through the bad spirits, all the elements of damning evil flow foully up and are appropriated by the freedom of the bad man.

The other kind of influx is called immediate. This is when the Lord himself, the pure substance of truth and good, flows into every organ and faculty of man. This influx is perpetual, but is received as truth and good only by the true and good. It is rejected, suffocated, or perverted by those who are in love with falsities and evils. So the light of the sun produces colors varying with the substances it falls on, and water takes forms corresponding to the vessels it is poured into.

The whole invisible world heaven, hell, and the middle state is peopled solely from the different families of the human race occupying the numerous material globes of the universe. The good, on leaving the fleshly body, are angels, the bad, demons. There is no angel nor demon who was created such at first. Satan is not a personality, but is a figurative term standing for the whole complex of hell. In the invisible world, time and space in one sense cease to be; in another sense they remain unchanged. They virtually cease because all our present measures of them are annihilated;11 they virtually remain because exact correspondences to them are left. To spirits, time is no longer measured by the revolution of planets, but by the succession of inward states; space is measured not by way marks and the traversing of distances, but by inward similitudes and dissimilitudes. Those who are unlike are sundered by gulfs of difference. Those who are alike are together in their interiors. Thought and love, forgetfulness and hate, are not hampered by temporal and spatial boundaries. Spiritual forces and beings spurn material impediments, and are united or separate, reciprocally visible or invisible, mutually conscious or unconscious, according to their own laws of kindred or alien adaptedness.

The soul the true man is its own organized and deathless body, and when it leaves its earthly house of flesh it knows the only resurrection, and the cast off frame returns to the dust forever. Swedenborg repeatedly affirms with emphasis that no one is born for hell, but that all are born for heaven, and that when any one comes into hell it is from his own free fault. He asserts that every infant, wheresoever born, whether within the Church or out of it, whether of pious parents or of impious, when he dies is received by the Lord, and educated in heaven, and becomes an angel. A central principle of which he never loses sight is that "a life of charity, which consists in acting sincerely and justly in every function, in every engagement, and in every work, from a heavenly motive, according to the Divine laws, is possible to every one, and infallibly leads to heaven." It does not matter whether the person leading such a life be a Christian or a Gentile. The only essential is that his ruling motive be divine and his life be in truth and good.

The Swedenborgian doctrine concerning Christ and his mission is that he was the infinite God incarnate, not incarnate for the purpose of expiating human sin and purchasing a ransom for the lost by vicarious sufferings, but for the sake of suppressing the rampant power of the hells, weakening the influx of the infernal spirits, setting an example to men, and revealing many important truths. The advantage of the Christian over the pagan is that the former is enlightened by the celestial knowledge contained in the Bible, and animated by the affecting motives presented in the drama of the Divine incarnation. There is no probation after this life. Just as one is on leaving the earth he goes into the spiritual world. There his

11 Philo the Jew says, (vol. i. p. 277, ed. Mangey,) "God is the Father of the world: the world is the father of time, begetting it by its own motion: time, therefore, holds the place of grandchild to God." But the world is only one measure of time; another, and a more important one, is the inward succession of the spirit's states of consciousness. Between Philo and Swedenborg, it may be remarked here, there are many remarkable correspondences both of thought and language. For example, Philo says, (vol. i. p. 494,) "Man is a small kosmos, the kosmos is a grand man."

ruling affection determines his destiny, and that affection can never be extirpated or changed to all eternity. After death, evil life cannot in any manner or degree be altered to good life, nor infernal love be transmuted to angelic love, inasmuch as every spirit from head to foot is in quality such as his love is, and thence such as his life is, so that to transmute this life into the opposite is altogether to destroy the spirit. It were easier, says Swedenborg, to change a night bird into a dove, an owl into a bird of paradise, than to change a subject of hell into a subject of heaven after the line of death has been crossed. But why the crossing of that line should make such an infinite difference he does not explain; nor does he prove it as a fact.

The moral reason and charitable heart of Swedenborg vehemently revolted from the Calvinistic doctrines of predestination and vicarious atonement, and the group of thoughts that cluster around them. He always protests against these dogmas, refutes them with varied power and consistency; and the leading principles of his own system are creditable to human nature, and attribute no unworthiness to the character of God. A debt of eternal gratitude is due to Swedenborg that his influence, certainly destined to be powerful and lasting, is so clearly calculated to advance the interests at once of philosophic intelligence, social affection, and true piety. The superiorities of his view of the future life over those which it seeks to supplant are weighty and numerous. The following may be reckoned among the most prominent.

First, without predicating of God any aggravated severity or casting the faintest shadow on his benevolence, it gives us the most appalling realization of the horribleness of sin and of its consequences. God is commonly represented in effect, at least as flaming with anger against sinners, and forcibly flinging them into the unappeasable fury of Tophet, where his infinite vengeance may forever satiate itself on them. But, Swedenborg says, God is incapable of hatred or wrath: he casts no one into hell; but the wicked go where they belong by their own election, from the inherent fitness and preference of their ruling love. The evil man desires to be in hell because there he finds his food, employment, and home; in heaven he would suffer unutterable agonies from every circumstance. The wicked go into hell by the necessary and benignant love of God, not by his indignation; and their retributions are in their own characters, not in their prison house. This does not flout and trample all magnanimity, nor shock the heart of piety; and yet, showing us men compelled to prefer wallowing in the filth and iniquities of hell, clinging to the very evils whose pangs transfix them, it gives us the direst of all the impressions of sin, and beneath the lowest deep of the popular hell opens to our shuddering conceptions a deep of loathsomeness immeasurably lower still.

Secondly, the Swedenborgian doctrine of the conditions of salvation or reprobation, when compared with the popular doctrine, is marked by striking depth of insight, justice, and liberality. Every man is free. Every man has power to receive the influx of truth and good from the Lord and convert it to its blessed and saving uses, piety towards God, good will towards the neighbor, and all kinds of right works. Who does this, no matter in what land or age he lives, becomes an heir of heaven. Who perverts those Divine gifts to selfishness and unrighteous deeds becomes a subject of hell. No mere opinion, no mere profession, no mere ritual services, no mere external obedience, not all these things together, can save a man, nor their absence condemn him; but the controlling motive of his life, the central and ruling love which constitutes the substance of his being, this decides every man's doom. The view is simple, reasonable, just, necessary. And so is the doctrine of degrees accompanying it; namely, that there are in heaven different grades and qualities of exaltation and delight, and in hell of degradation and woe, for different men according to their capacities and deserts. A profoundly ethical character pervades the scheme, and the great stamp of law is over it all.

Thirdly, a manifest advantage of Swedenborg's doctrine over the popular doctrine is the intimate connection it establishes between the present and the future, the visible and the invisible, God and man. Heaven and hell are not distant localities, entrance into which is to be won or avoided by moral artifices or sacramental subterfuges, but they are states of being depending on personal goodness or evil. God is not throned at the heart or on the apex of the universe, where at some remote epoch we hope to go and see him, but he is the Life feeding our lives freshly every instant. The spiritual world, with all its hosts, sustains and arches, fills and envelops us. Death is the dropping of the outer body, the lifting of an opaque veil, and we are among the spirits, unchanged, as we were before. Judgment is not a tribunal dawning on the close of the world's weary centuries, but the momentary assimilation of a celestial or an infernal love leading to states and acts, rewards and retributions, corresponding. Before this view the dead universe becomes a live transparency overwritten with the will, tremulous with the breath, and irradiate with the illumination of God.

We cannot but regret that the Swedenborgian view of the future life should be burdened and darkened with the terrible error of the dogma of eternal damnation, spreading over the state of all the subjects of the hells the pall of immitigable hopelessness, denying that they can ever make the slightest ameliorating progress. We have never been able to see force enough in any of the arguments or assertions advanced in support of this tremendous horror to warrant the least hesitation in rejecting it. For ourselves, we must regard it as incredible, and think that God cannot permit it. Instruction, reformation, progress, are the final aims of punishment. Aspiration is the concomitant of consciousness, and the authentic voice of God. Surely, sooner or later, in the boonful eternities of being, every creature capable of intelligence, allied to the moral law, drawing life from the Infinite, must begin to travel the ascending path of virtue and blessedness, and never retrograde again.

Neither can we admit in general the claim made by Swedenborg and by his disciples that the way in which he arrived at his system of theology elevates it to the rank of a Divine revelation. It is asserted that God opened his interior vision, so that he saw what had hitherto been concealed from the eyes of men in the flesh, namely, the inhabitants, laws, contents, and experiences of the spiritual world, and thus that his statements are not speculations or arguments, but records of unerring knowledge, his descriptions not fanciful pictures of the imagination, but literal transcripts of the truth he saw. This, in view of the great range of known experience, is not intrinsically probable, and we have seen no proof of it. Judging from what we know of psychological and religious history, it is far more likely that a man should confound his intangible reveries with solid fact than that he should be inspired by God to reveal a world of mysterious truths. Furthermore, while we are impressed with the reasonableness, probability, and consistency of most of the general principles of Swedenborg's exposition of the future life, we cannot but shrink from many of the details and forms in which he carries them out. Notwithstanding the earnest avowals of able disciples of his school that all his details are strictly necessitated by his premises, and that all his premises are laws of truth, we are compelled to regard a great many of his assertions as purely arbitrary and a great many of his descriptions as purely fanciful. But, denying that his scheme of eschatology is a scientific representation of the reality, and looking at it as a poetic structure reared by co working knowledge and imagination on the ground of reason, nature, and morality, whose foundation walls, columns, and grand outlines are truth, while many of its details, ornaments, and images are fancy, it must be acknowledged to be one of the most wonderful examples of creative power extant in the literature of the world. No one who has mastered it with appreciative mind will question this. There are, expressed and latent, in the totality of Swedenborg's accounts of hell and heaven, more variety of imagery, power of moral truth and appeal, exhibition of dramatic justice, transcendent delights of holiness and love, curdling terrors of evil and woe, strength of philosophical grasp, and sublimity of emblematic conception, than are to be found in Dante's earth renowned poem. We say this of the substance of his ideas, not of the shape and clothing in which they are represented. Swedenborg was no poet in language and form, only in conception.

Take this picture. In the topmost height of the celestial world the Lord appears as a sun, and all the infinite multitudes of angels, swarming up through the innumerable heavens, wherever they are, continually turn their faces towards him in love and joy. But at the bottom of the infernal world is a vast ball of blackness, towards which all the hosts of demons, crowding down through the successive hells, forever turn their eager faces away from God. Or consider this. Every thing consists of a great number of perfect leasts like itself: every heart is an aggregation of little hearts, every lung an aggregation of little lungs, every eye an aggregation of little eyes. Following out the principle, every society in the spiritual world is a group of spirits arranged in the form of a man, every heaven is a gigantic man composed of an immense number of individuals, and all the heavens together constitute one Grand Man, a countless number of the most intelligent angels forming the head, a stupendous organization of the most affectionate making the heart, the most humble going to the feet, the most useful attracted to the hands, and so on through every part.

With exceptions, then, we regard Swedenborg's doctrine of the future life as a free poetic presentment, not as a severe scientific statement, of views true in moral principle, not of facts real in literal detail. His imagination and sentiment are mathematical and ethical instead of asthetic and passionate. Milk seems to run in his veins instead of blood, but he is of truthfulness and charity all compact. We think it most probable that the secret of his supposed inspiration was the abnormal frequent or chronic turning of his mind into what is called the ecstatic or clairvoyant state. This condition being spontaneously induced, while he yet, in some unexplained manner, retained conscious possession and control of his usual faculties, he treated his subjective conceptions as objective realities, believed his interior contemplations were accurate visions of facts, and took the strange

This hypothesis, taken in conjunction with the comprehensiveness of his mind, the vastness of his learning, the integral correctness of his conscience, and his disciplined habits of thought, will go far towards explaining the unparalleled phenomenon of his theological works; and, though it leaves many things unaccounted for, it seems to us more credible than any other which has yet been suggested.

The last of the three prominent phenomena which as before said followed the Protestant Reformation was rationalism, an attempt to try all religious questions at the tribunal of reason and by the tests of conscience. The great movement led by Luther was but one element in a numerous train of influences and events all yielding their different contributions to that resolute rationalistic tendency which afterwards broke out so powerfully in England, France, and Germany, and, spreading thence into every country in Christendom, has been, in secret and in public, with slow, sure steps, irresistibly advancing ever since. In the history of scholasticism there were three distinct epochs. The first period was characterized by the servile submission and conformity of philosophy to the theology dictated by the Church. The second period was marked by the formal alliance and attempted reconciliation of philosophy and theology. The third period saw an ever increasing jealousy and separation between the philosophers and the theologians.12 Many an adventurous thinker pushed his speculations beyond the limits of the established theology, and deliberately dissented from the orthodox standards in his conclusions. Perhaps Abelard, who openly strove to put all the Church dogmas in forms acceptable to philosophy, and who did not hesitate to reject in many instances what seemed to him unreasonable, deserves to be called the father of rationalism. The works of Des Cartes, Leibnitz, Wolf, Kant's "Religion within the Bounds of Pure Reason," together with the influence and the writings of many other eminent philosophers, gradually gave momentum to the impulse and popularity to the habits of free thought and criticism even in the realm of theology. The dogmatic scheme of the dominant Church was firmly seized, many errors shaken out to the light and exposed, and many long received opinions questioned and flung into doubt.13 The authenticity of many of the popular doctrines regarding the future life could not fail to be denied as soon as it was attempted as was extensively done about the middle of the eighteenth century to demonstrate them by mathematical methods, with all the array of axioms, theorems, lemmas, doubts, and solutions. Flugge has historically illustrated the employment of this method at considerable length.14

12 Cousin, Hist. Mod. Phil., lect. ix.

13 Staudlin, Geschichte des Rationalismus. Saintes, Histoire Critique du Rationalisme en Allemagne, Eng. trans. by Dr. Beard.

14 Geschichte des Glaubens an Unsterblichkeit, u. s. f., th. iii. abth. ii. ss. 281-289.

The essence of rationalism is the affirmation that neither the Fathers, nor the Church, nor the Scriptures, nor all of them together, can rightfully establish any proposition opposed to the logic of sound philosophy, the principles of reason, and the evident truth of nature. Around this thesis the battle has been fought and the victory won; and it will stand with spreading favor as long as there are unenslaved and cultivated minds in the world. This position is, in logical necessity, and as a general thing in fact, that of the large though loosely cohering body of believers known as "Liberal Christians;" and it is tacitly held by still larger and ever growing numbers nominally connected with sects that officially eschew it with horror. The result of the studies and discussions associated with this principle, so far as it relates to the subject before us, has been the rejection of the following popular doctrines: the plenary inspiration of the Scriptures as an ultimate authority in matters of belief; unconditional predestination; the satisfaction theory of the vicarious atonement; the visible second coming of Christ, in person, to burn up the world and to hold a general judgment; the intermediate state of souls; the resurrection of the body; a local hell of material fire in the bowels of the earth; the eternal damnation of the wicked. These old dogmas,15 scarcely changed, still remain in the stereotyped creeds of all the prominent denominations; but they slumber there to an astonishing extent unrealized, unnoticed, unthought of, by the great multitude of common believers, while every consciously rational investigator vehemently repudiates them. To every candid mind that has really studied their nature and proofs their absurdity is now transparent on all the grounds alike of history, metaphysics, morals, and science.

The changes of the popular Christian belief in regard to three salient points have been especially striking. First, respecting the immediate fate of the dead, an intermediate state. The predominant Jewish doctrine was that all souls went indiscriminately into a sombre under world, where they awaited a resurrection.

The earliest Christian view prevalent was the same, with the exception that it divided that place of departed spirits into two parts, a painful for the bad, a pleasant for the good. The next opinion that prevailed the Roman Catholic was the same as the foregoing, with two exceptions: it established a purgatory in addition to the previous paradise and hell, and it opened heaven itself for the immediate entrance of a few spotless souls. Pope John XXII., as Gieseler shows, was accused of heresy by the theological doctors of Paris because he declared that no soul could enter heaven and enjoy the beatific vision until after the resurrection. Pope Benedict XII. drew up a list of one hundred and seventeen heretical opinions held by the Armenian Christians. One of these notions was that the souls of all deceased adults wander in the air until the Day of Judgment, neither hell, paradise, nor heaven being open to them until after that day. Thomas Aquinas says, "Each soul at death immediately flies to its appointed place, whether in hell or in heaven, being without the body until the resurrection, with it afterwards."16 Then came the

15 They are defended in all their literal grossness in the two following works, both recent publications. The World to Come; by the Rev. James Cochrane. Der Tod, das Todtenreich, und der Zustand der abgeschiedenen Seelen; von P. A. Maywahlen.

16 Summa iii. in Suppl. 69. 2.

dogma of the orthodox Protestants, slightly varying in the different sects, but generally agreeing that at death all redeemed souls pass instantly to heaven and all unredeemed souls to hell.17 The principal variation from this among believers within the Protestant fellowship has been the notion that the souls of all men die or sleep with the body until the Day of Judgment, a notion which peeps out here and there in superstitious spots along the pages of ecclesiastical history, and which has found now and then an advocate during the last century and a half. The Council of Elvin, in Spain, forbade the lighting of tapers in churchyards, lest it should disturb the souls of the deceased buried there. At this day, in prayers and addresses at funerals, no phrases are more common than those alluding to death as a sleep, and implying that the departed one is to slumber peacefully in his grave until the resurrection. And yet, at the same time, by the same persons contrary ideas are frequently expressed. The truth is, the subject, owing to the contradictions between their creed and their reason, is left by most persons in hopeless confusion and uncertainty. They have no determinately reconciled and conscious views of their own. Rationalism sweeps away all the foregoing incongruous medley at once, denying that we know any thing about the precise localities of heaven and hell, or the destined order of events in the hidden future of separate souls; affirming that all we should dare to say is simply that the souls whether of good or of bad men, on leaving the body, go at once into a spiritual state of being, where they will live immortally, as God decrees, never returning to be reinvested with the vanished charnel houses of clay they once inhabited.

Secondly, the thought that Christ after his death descended into the under world to ransom mankind, or a part of mankind, from the doom there, is in the foundation of the apostolic theology. It was a central element in the belief of the Fathers, and of the Church for fourteen hundred years. None of the prominent Protestant reformers thought of denying it. Calvin lays great stress on it.18 Apinus and others, at Hamburg, maintained that Christ's descent was a part of his humiliation, and that in it he suffered unutterable pains for us. On the other hand, Melancthon and the Wittenbergers held that the descent was a part of Christ's triumph, since by it he won a glorious victory over the powers of hell.19 But gradually the importance and the redeeming effects attached to Christ's descent into hell were transferred to his death on the cross. Slowly the primitive dogma dwindled away, and finally sunk out of sight, through an ever encroaching disbelief in the physical conditions on which it rested and in the pictorial environments by which it was recommended. And now it is scarcely ever heard of, save when brought out from old scholastic tomes by some theological delver. Baumgarten Crusius has learnedly illustrated the important place long held by this notion, and well shown its gradual retreat into the unnoticed background.20

17 Confession of Faith of the Church of Scotland, ch. xxxii. Calvin, Institutes, lib. iii. cap. xxv.; and his Psychopannychia. Quenstedt also affirms it. Likewise the Confession of Faith of the Westminster Divines, art.

xxxii., says, "Souls neither die nor sleep, but go immediately to heaven or hell."

18 Institutes, lib. ii. cap. 16, sects. 16, 19.

19 Ledderhose, Life of Melancthon, Eng. trans. by Krotel, ch. xxx.

20 Compendium der Christliche Dogmengeschichte, thl. ii. sects. 100-109.

The other particular doctrine which we said had undergone remarkable change is in regard to the number of the saved. A blessed improvement has come over the popular Christian feeling and teaching in respect to this momentous subject. The Jews excluded from salvation all but their own strict ritualists. The apostles, it is true, excluded none but the stubbornly wicked. But the majority of the Fathers virtually allowed the possibility of salvation to few indeed. Chrysostom doubted if out of the hundred thousand souls constituting the Christian population of Antioch in his day one hundred would be saved! 21 And when we read, with shuddering soul, the calculations of Cornelius a Lapide, or the celebrated sermon of Massillon on the "Small Number of the Saved," we are compelled to confess that they fairly represent the almost universal sentiment and conviction of Christendom for more than seventeen hundred years. A quarto volume published in London in 1680, by Du Moulin, called "Moral Reflections upon the Number of the Elect," affirmed that not one in a million, from Adam down to our times, shall be saved. A flaming execration blasted the whole heathen world, 22 and a metaphysical quibble doomed ninety nine of every hundred in Christian lands. Collect the whole relevant theological literature of the Christian ages, from the birth of Tertullian to the death of Jonathan Edwards, strike the average pitch of its doctrinal temper, and you will get this result: that in the field of human souls Satan is the harvester,

God the gleaner; hell receives the whole vintage in its wine press of damnation, heaven obtains only a few straggling clusters plucked for salvation. The crowded wains roll staggering into the iron doorways of Satan's fire and brimstone barns; the redeemed vestiges of the world crop of men are easily borne to heaven in the arms of a few weeping angels. How different is the prevailing tone of preaching and belief now! What a cheerful ascent of views from the mournful passage of the dead over the river of oblivion fancied by the Greeks, or the excruciating passage of the river of fire painted by the Catholics, to the happy passage of the river of balm, healing every weary bruise and sorrow, promised by the Universalists! It is true, the old harsh exclusiveness is still organically imbedded in the established creeds, all of which deny the possibility of salvation beyond the little circle who vitally appropriate the vicarious atonement of Christ; but then this is, for the most part, a dead letter in the creeds. In the hearts and in the candid confessions of all but one in a thousand it is discredited and sincerely repelled as an abomination to human nature, a reflection against God, an outrage upon the substance of ethics. Remorseless bigots may gloat and exult over the thought that those who reject their dogmas shall be thrust into the roaring fire gorges of hell; but a better spirit is the spirit of the age we live in; and, doubtless, a vast majority of the men we daily meet really believe that all who try to the best of their ability, according to their light and circumstances, to do what is right, in the love of God and man, shall be saved. In that moving scene of the great dramatist where the burial of the innocent and hapless Ophelia is represented, and Lacrtes vainly seeks to win from the Church official

21 In Acta Apostolorum, homil. xxiv.

22 Gotze, Ueber die Neue Meinung von der Seligkeit der angeblich guten und redlichen Seelen unter Juden, Heiden, und Turken durch Christum, ohne dass sie an ihn glauben.

the full funeral rites of religion over her grave, the priest may stand for the false and cruel ritual spirit, the brother for the just and native sentiment of the human heart. Says the priest, "We should profane the service of the dead To sing a requiem and such rest to her As to peace parted souls." And Laertes replies, "Lay her in the earth; And from her fair and unpolluted flesh Shall violets spring. I tell thee, churlish priest, A ministering angel shall my sister be When thou liest howling."

Indeed, who that has a heart in his bosom would not be ashamed not to sympathize with the gentle hearted Burns when he expresses even to the devil himself the quaint and kindly wish, "Oh wad ye tak' a thought and mend!"

The creeds and the priests, in congenial alliance with many evil things, may strive to counteract this progressive self emancipation from cruel falsehoods and superstitions, but in vain. The terms of salvation are seen lying in the righteous will of a gracious God, not in the heartless caprice of a priesthood nor in the iron gripe of a set of dogmas. The old priestly monopoly over the way to heaven has been taken off in the knowledge of the enlightened present, and, for all who have unfettered feet to walk with, the passage to God is now across a free bridge. The ancient exactors may still sit in their toll house creeds and confessionals; but their authority is gone, and the virtuous traveller, stepping from the ground of time upon the planks that lead over into eternity, smiles as he passes scot free by their former taxing terrors.

The reign of sacramentalists and dogmatists rapidly declines. Reason, common sentiment, the liberal air, the best and strongest tendencies of the people, are against them to day, and will be more against them in every coming day. Every successive explosion of the Second Adventist fanaticism will leave less of that element behind. Its rage in America, under the auspices of Miller, in the nineteenth century, was tame and feeble when compared with the terror awakened in Europe in the fifteenth century by Stofler's prediction of an approaching comet.23 Every new discovery of the harmonies of science, and of the perfections of nature, and of the developments of the linear logic of God consistently unfolding in implicated sequences of peaceful order unperturbed by shocks of failure and epochs of remedy, will increase and popularize an intelligent faith in the original ordination and the intended permanence of the present constitution of things. Finally men will cease to be looking up to see the blue dome cleave open for the descent of angelic squadrons headed by the majestic Son of God, the angry breath of his mouth consuming the world, cease to

23 Bayle, Historical Dictionary, art. Stofler, note B.

expect salvation by any other method than that of earnest and devout truthfulness, love, good works, and pious submissiveness to God, cease to fancy that their souls, after waiting through the long sleep or separation of death, will return and take on their old bodies again. Recognizing the Divine plan for training souls in this lower and transient state for a higher and immortal state, they will endeavor, in natural piety and mutual love, while they live, to exhaust the genuine uses of the world that now is, and thus prepare themselves to enter with happiest auspices, when they die, the world prepared for them beyond these mortal shores.

These cheerful prophecies must be verified in the natural course of things. The rapid spread of the doctrine of a future life taught by the "Spirit rappers" is a remarkable revelation of the great extent to which the minds of the common people have at last become free from the long domination of the ecclesiastical dogmas on that subject. The leading representatives of the "Spiritualists" affirm, with much unanimity, the most comforting conclusions as to the condition of the departed. They exclude all wrath and favoritism from the disposition of the Deity. They have little in fact, they often have nothing whatever to say of hell. They emphatically repudiate the ordinarily taught terms of salvation, and deny the doctrine of hopeless reprobation. All death is beautiful and progressive. "Every form and thing is constantly growing lovelier and every sphere purer." The abode of each soul in the future state is determined, not by decrees or dogmas or forms of any kind, but by qualities of character, degrees of love, purity, and wisdom. There are seven ascending spheres, each more abounding than the one below it in beauties, glories, and happiness. "The first sphere is the natural; the second, the spiritual; the third, the celestial; the fourth, the supernatural; the fifth, the superspiritual; the sixth, the supercelestial; the seventh, the Infinite Vortex of Love and Wisdom."[24] Whatever be thought of the pretensions of this doctrine to be a Divine revelation, whatever be thought of its various psychological, cosmological, and theological characteristics, its ethics are those of natural reason. It is wholly irreconcilable with the popular ecclesiastical system of doctrines. Its epidemic diffusion until now burdened as it is with such nauseating accompaniments of crudity and absurdity, it reckons its adherents by millions is a tremendous evidence of the looseness with which the old, cruel dogmas sit on the minds of the masses of the people, and of their eager readiness to welcome more humane views.

In science the erroneous doctrines of the Middle Age are now generally discarded. The mention of them but provokes a smile or awakens surprise. Yet, as compared with the historic annals of our race, it is but recently that the true order of the solar system has been unveiled, the weight of the air discovered, the circulation of the blood made known, the phenomena of insanity intelligently studied, the results of physiological chemistry brought to light, the symmetric domain and sway of calculable law pushed far out in every direction of nature and experience. It used to be supposed that digestion was effected by means of a mechanical power equal to many tons. Borelli asserted that the muscular force of the heart was one hundred and eighty thousand pounds. These absurd estimates only disappeared when the

24 Andrew Jackson Davis, Nature's Divine Revelations, sects. 192 203.

properties of the gastric juice were discerned. The method in which we distinguish the forms and distances of objects was not understood until Berkeley published his "New Theory of Vision." Few persons are aware of the opposition of bigotry, stolidity, and authority against which the brilliant advances of scientific discovery and mechanical invention and social improvement have been forced to contend, and in despite of which they have slowly won their way. Excommunications, dungeons, fires, sneers, polite persecution, bitter neglect, tell the story, from the time the Athenians banned Anaxagoras for calling the sun a mass of fire, to the day an English mob burned the warehouses of Arkwright because he had invented the spinning jenny. But, despite all the hostile energies of establishment, prejudice, and scorn, the earnest votaries of philosophical truth have studied and toiled with ever accumulating victories, until now a hundred sciences are ripe with emancipating fruits and perfect freedom to be taught. Railroads gird the lands with ribs of trade, telegraphs thread the airs with electric tidings of events, and steamships crease the seas with channels of foam and fire. There is no longer danger of any one being put to death, or even being excluded from the "best society," for saying that the earth moves. An eclipse cannot be regarded as the frown of God when it is regularly foretold with certainty. The measurement of the atmosphere exterminated the wiseacre proverb, "Nature abhors a vacuum," by the burlesque addition, "but only for the first thirty two feet." The madman cannot be looked on as divinely inspired, his words to be caught as oracles, or as possessed by a devil, to be chained and scourged, since Pinel's great work has brought insanity within the range of organic disease. When Franklin's kite drew electricity from the cloud to his knuckle, the superstitious theory of thunder died a natural death.

The vast progress effected in all departments of physical science during the last four centuries has not been made in any kindred degree in the prevailing theology. Most of the harsh, unreasonable tenets of the elaborately morbid and distorted mediaval theologyare still retained in the creeds of the great majority of Christendom. The causes of this difference are plain. The establishment of newly discovered truths in material science being less intimately connected with the prerogatives of the ruling classes, less clearly hostile to the permanence of their power, they have not offered so pertinacious an opposition to progress in this province: they have yielded a much larger freedom to physicists than to moralists, to discoverers of mathematical, chemical, and mechanical law than to reformers of political and religious thought. Livy tells us that, in the five hundred and seventy third year of Rome, some concealed books of Numa were found, which, on examination by the priests, being thought injurious to the established religion, were ordered to be burned.25 The charge was not that they were ungenuine, nor that their contents were false; but they were dangerous. In the second century, an imperial decree forbade the reading of the Sibylline Oracles, because they contained prophecies of Christ and doctrines of Christianity. By an act of the English Parliament, in the middle of the seventeenth century, every copy of the Racovian Catechism (an exposition of the Socinian doctrine) that could be obtained was burned in the streets.

25 Lib. xl. cap. xxix.

The Index Expurgatorius for Catholic countries is still freshly filled every year. And in Protestant countries a more subtle and a more effectual influence prevents, on the part of the majority, the candid perusal of all theological discussions which are not pitched in the orthodox key. Certain dogmas are the absorbed thought of the sects which defend them: no fresh and independent thinking is to be expected on those subjects, no matter how purely fictitious these secretions of the brain of the denomination or of some ancient leader may be, no matter how glaringly out of keeping with the intelligence and liberty which reign in other realms of faith and feeling. There is nowhere else in the world a tyranny so pervasive and despotic as that which rules in the department of theological opinion. The prevalent slothful and slavish surrender of the grand privileges and duties of individual thought, independent personal conviction and action in religious matters, is at once astonishing, pernicious, and disgraceful. The effect of entrenched tradition, priestly directors, a bigoted, overawing, and persecuting sectarianism, is nowhere else a hundredth part so powerful or so extensive.

In addition to the bitter determination by interested persons to suppress reforming investigations of the doctrines which hold their private prejudices in supremacy, and to the tremendous social prestige of old establishment, another cause has been active to keep theology stationary while science has been making such rapid conquests. Science deals with tangible quantities, theology with abstract qualities. The cultivation of the former yields visible practical results of material comfort; the cultivation of the latter yields only inward spiritual results of mental welfare. Accordingly, science has a thousand resolute votaries where theology has one unshackled disciple. At this moment, a countless multitude, furnished with complex apparatus, are ransacking every nook of nature, and plucking trophies, and the world with honoring attention reads their reports. But how few with competent preparation and equipment, with fearless consecration to truth, unhampered, with fresh free vigor, are scrutinizing the problems of theology, enthusiastically bent upon refuting errors and proving verities! And what reception do the conclusions of those few meet at the hands of the public?

Surely not prompt recognition, frank criticism, and grateful acknowledgment or courteous refutation. No; but studied exclusion from notice, or sophistical evasions and insulting vituperation.

What a striking and painful contrast is afforded by the generous encouragement given to the students of science by the annual bestowment of rewards by the scientific societies such as the Cuvier Prize, the Royal Medal, the Rumford Medal and the jealous contempt and assaults visited by the sectarian authorities upon those earnest students of theology who venture to propose any innovating improvement! Suppose there were annually awarded an Aquinas Prize, a Fenelon Medal, a Calvin Medal, a Luther Medal, a Channing Medal, not to the one who should present the most ingenious defence of any peculiar tenet of one of those masters, but to him who should offer the most valuable fresh contribution to theological truth! What should we think if the French Institute offered a gold medal every year to the astronomer who presented the ablest essay in support of the Ptolemaic system, or if the Royal Society voted a diploma for the best method of casting nativities? Such is the course pursued in regard to dogmatic theology. The consequence has been that while elsewhere the ultimate standard by which to try a doctrine is, What do the most competent judges say? What does unprejudiced reason dictate? What does the great harmony of truth require? in theology it is, What do the committed priests say? How does it comport with the old traditions?

We read in the Hak ul Yakeen that the envoy of Herk, Emperor of Rum, once said to the prophet, "You summon people to a Paradise whose extent includes heaven and earth: where, then, is hell?" Mohammed replied, "When day comes, where is night?" That is to say, according to the traditionary glosses, as day and night are opposite, so Paradise is at the zenith and hell at the nadir. Yes; but if Paradise be above the heavens, and hell below the seventh earth, then how can Sirat be extended over hell for people to pass to Paradise? "We reply," say the authors of the Hak ul Yakeen, "that speculation on this subject is not necessary, nor to be regarded. Implicit faith in what the prophets have revealed must be had; and explanatory surmises, which are the occasion of Satanic doubts, must not be indulged."26 Certainly this exclusion of reason cannot always be suffered. It is fast giving way already. And it is inevitable that, when reason secures its right and bears its rightful fruits in moral subjects as it now does in physical subjects, the mediaval theology must be rejected as mediaval science has been. It is the common doctrine of the Church that Christ now sits in heaven in a human body of flesh and blood. Calvin separated the Divine nature of Christ from this human body; but Luther made the two natures inseparable and attributed ubiquity to the body in which they reside, thus asserting the omnipresence of a material human body, a bulk of a hundred and fifty pounds' weight more or less. He furiously assailed Zwingle's objection to this monstrous nonsense, as "a devil's mask and grandchild of that old witch, mistress Reason." 27 The Roman Church teaches, and her adherents devoutly believe, that the house of the Virgin Mary was conveyed on the wings of angels from Nazareth to the eastern slope of the Apennines above the Adriatic Gulf.28 The English Church, consistently interpreted, teaches that there is no salvation without baptism by priests in the line of apostolic succession. These are but ordinary specimens of teachings still humbly received by the mass of Christians. The common distrust with which the natural operations of reason are regarded in the Church, the extreme reluctance to accept the conclusions of mere reason, seem to us discreditable to the theological leaders who represent the current creeds of the approved sects. Many an influential theologian could learn invaluable lessons from the great guides in the realm of science. The folly which acute learned wise men will be guilty of the moment they turn to theological subjects, where they do not allow reason to act, is both ludicrous and melancholy. The victim of lycanthropy used to be burned alive; he is now placed under the careful treatment of skilful and humane physicians. But the heretic or infidel is still thought to be inspired by the devil, a fit subject for discipline here and hell hereafter. The light shed abroad by the rising spirit of rational investigation must gradually dispel the delusions which lurk in the vales of theology, as it already has dispelled those that formerly haunted the hills of science. The spectres which have so long terrified a childish world will successively vanish

26 Merrick, Hyat ul Kuloob, note 74.

27 Hagenbach, Dogmengeschichte, sect. 265, note 2.

28 Christian Remembrancer, April, 1855. A full and able history of the "Holy House of Loretto."

from the path of man as advancing reason, in the name of the God of truth, utters its imperial "Avaunt!"

Henry More wrote a book on the "Immortality of the Soul," printed in London in 1659, just two hundred years ago. It is full of beauty, acumen, and power. He was one of the first men of the time. Yet he seriously elaborates an argument like this: "The scum and spots that lie on the sun are as great an Argument that there is no Divinity in him as the dung of Owls and Sparrows that is found on the faces and shoulders of Idols in Temples are clear evidences that they are no true Deities."[29] He also in good faith tells a story like this: "That a Woman with child, seeing a Butcher divide a Swine's head with a Cleaver, brought forth her Child with its face cloven in the upper jaw, the palate, and upper lip to the very nose."[30] The progress marked by the contrast of the scientific spirit of the present time with the ravenous credulity of even two centuries back must continue and spread into every province. Some may vilify it; but in vain. Some may sophisticate against it; but in vain. Some may invoke authority and social persecution to stop it; but in vain. Some may appeal to the prejudices and fears of the timid; but in vain. Some may close their own eyes, and hold their hands before their neighbors' eyes, and attempt to shut out the light; but in vain. It will go on. It is the interest of the world that it should go on. It is the manly and the religious course to help this progress with prudence and reverence. Truth is the will of God, the way he has made things to be and to act, the way he wishes free beings to exist and to act. He has ordained the gradual discovery of truth. And despite the struggles of selfish tyranny, and the complacence of luxurious ease, and the terror of ignorant cowardice, truth will be more and more brought to universal acceptance. Some men have fancied their bodies composed of butter or of glass; but when compelled to move out into the sunlight or the crowd they did not melt nor break.31 Esquirol had a patient who did not dare to bend her thumb, lest the world should come to an end. When forced to bend it, she was surprised that the crack of doom did not follow.

The mechanico theatrical character of the popular theology is enough to reveal its origin and its fundamental falsity. The difference between its lurid and phantasmal details and the calm eternal verities in the divinely constituted order of nature is as great as the difference between those stars which one sees in consequence of a blow on the forehead and those he sees by turning his gaze to the nightly sky. To every competent thinker, the bare appreciation of such a passage as that which closes Chateaubriand's chapter on the Last Judgment, with the huge bathos of its incongruous mixture of sublime and absurd, is its sufficient refutation: "The globe trembles on its axis; the moon is covered with a bloody veil; the threatening stars hang half detached from the vault of heaven, and the agony of the world commences. Now resounds the trump of the angel. The sepulchres burst: the human race issues all at once, and fills the Valley of Jehoshaphat! The Son of Man appears in the clouds; the powers of hell ascend from the infernal depths;

the goats are separated from the sheep; the wicked are plunged into the gulf; the just ascend to heaven; God returns to his repose,

29 Preface, p. 10.

30 Ibid. p. 392.

31 Bucknill and Tuke, Psychological Medicine, ch. ix.

and the reign of eternity begins."32 Nothing saves this whole scheme of doctrine from instant rejection except neglect of thought, or incompetence of thought, on the part of those who contemplate it. The peculiar dogmas of the exclusive sects are the products of mental and social disease, psychological growths in pathological moulds. The naked shapes of beautiful women floating around St. Anthony in full display of their maddening charms are interpreted by the Romanist Church as a visible work of the devil. An intelligent physician accounts for them by the laws of physiology, the morbid action of morbid nerves. There is no doubt whatever as to which of these explanations is correct. The absolute prevalence of that explanation is merely a question of time. Meanwhile, it is the part of every wise and devout man, without bigotry, without hatred for any, with strict fidelity to his own convictions, with entire tolerance and kindness for all who differ from him, sacredly to seek after verity himself and earnestly to endeavor to impart it to others. To such men forms of opinion, instead of being prisons, fetters, and barriers, will be but as tents of a night while they march through life, the burning and cloudy column of inquiry their guide, the eternal temple of truth their goal.

The actual relation, the becoming attitude, the appropriate feeling, of man towards the future state, the concealed segment of his destiny, are impressively shown in the dying scene of one of the wisest and most gifted of men, one of the fittest representatives of the modern mind. In a good old age, on a pleasant spring day, with a vast expanse of experience behind him, with an immensity of hope before him, he lay calmly expiring.

"More light!" he cried, with departing breath; and Death, solemn warder of eternity, led him, blinded, before the immemorial veil of awe and secrets. It uprolled as the flesh bandage fell from his spirit, and he walked at large, triumphant or appalled, amidst the unimagined revelations of God.

And now, recalling the varied studies we have passed through, and seeking for the conclusion or root of the matter, what shall we say? This much we will say. First, the fearless Christian, fully acquainted with the results of a criticism unsparing as the requisitions of truth and candor, can scarcely, with intelligent honesty, do more than place his hand on the beating of his heart, and fix his eye on the riven tomb of Jesus, and exclaim, "Feeling here the inspired promise of immortality, and seeing there the sign of God's authentic seal, I gratefully believe that Christ has risen, and that my soul is deathless!" Secondly, the trusting philosopher, fairly weighing the history of the world's belief in a future life, and the evidences on which it rests, can scarcely, with justifying warrant, do less than lay his hand on his body, and turn his gaze aloft, and exclaim, "Though death shatters this shell, the soul may survive, and I confidently hope to live forever." Meanwhile, the believer and the speculator, combining to form a Christian philosophy wherein doubt and faith, thought and freedom, reason and sentiment, nature and revelation, all embrace, even as the truth of things and the experience of life demand, may both adopt for their own the expression wrought for himself by a pure and fervent poet in these freighted lines of pathetic beauty:

32 Genius of Christianity, part ii. book vi. ch. vii.

"I gather up the scattered rays Of wisdom in the early days, Faint gleams and broken, like the light Of meteors in a Northern night, Betraying to the darkling earth The unseen sun which gave them birth; I listen to the sibyl's chant, The voice of priest and hierophant; I know what Indian Kreeshna saith, And what of life and what of death The demon taught to Socrates, And what, beneath his garden trees Slow pacing, with a dream like tread, The solemn thoughted Plato said; Nor Lack I tokens, great or small, Of God's clear light in each and all, While holding with more dear regard Than scroll of heathen seer and bard The starry pages, promise lit, With Christ's evangel overwrit, Thy miracle of life and death, O Holy One of Nazareth!"

www.ingramcontent.com/pod-product-compliance
Lightning Source LLC
Chambersburg PA
CBHW081728100526
44591CB00016B/2547